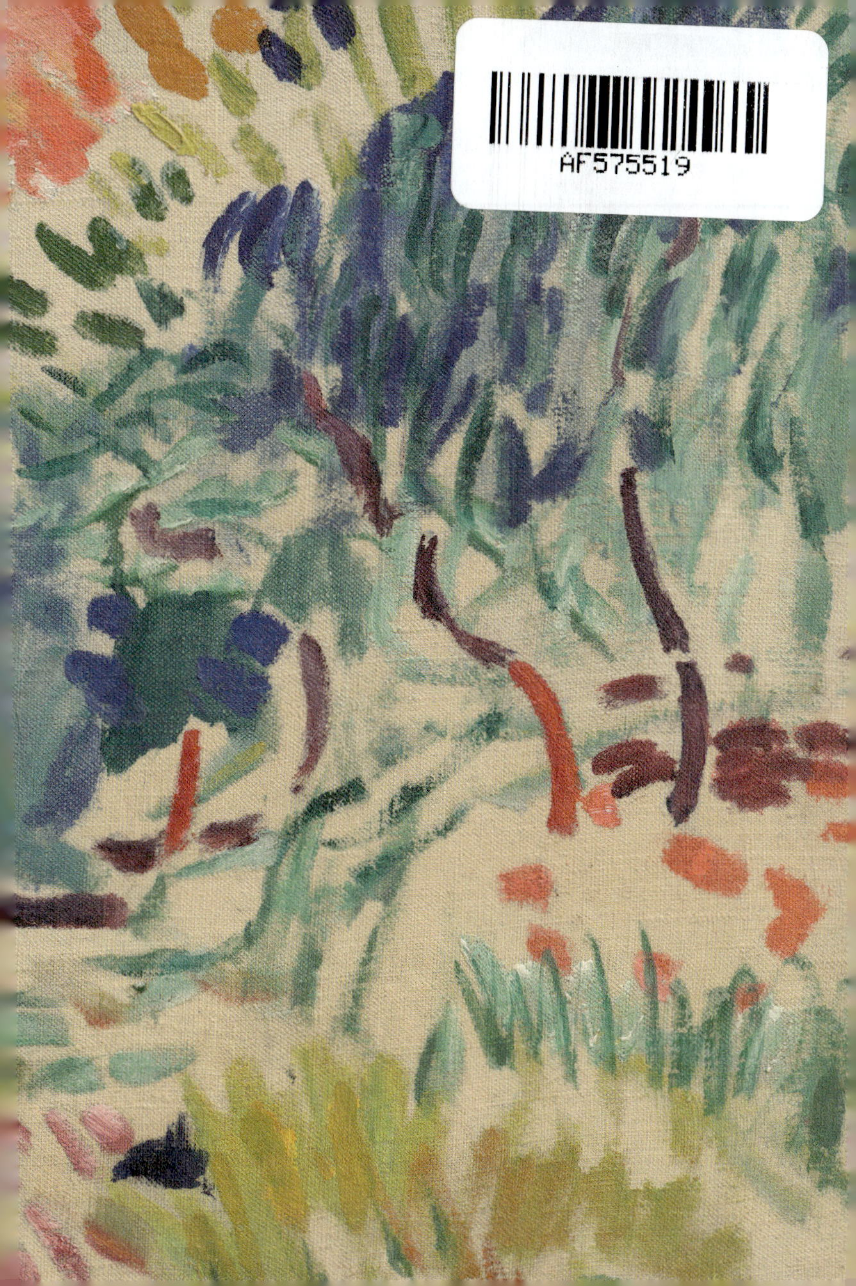

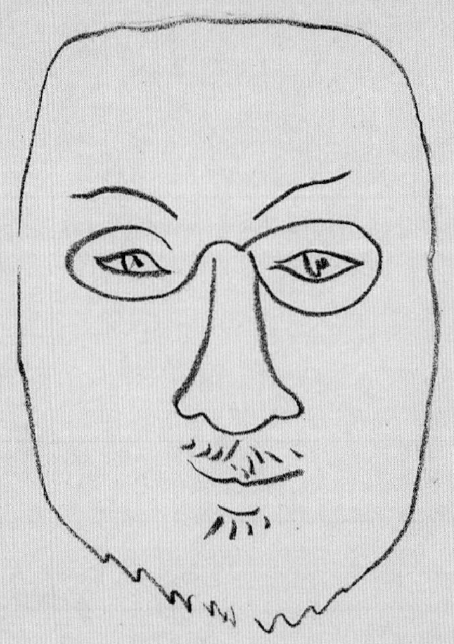
H Matisse
à André Rouveyre

THE WORLD
ACCORDING TO

MATISSE

Selected, with an introduction, by

Louise Rogers Lalaurie

with 70 illustrations

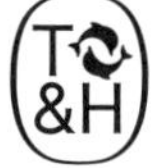

First published in the United Kingdom in 2026 by
Thames & Hudson Ltd, 6–24 Britannia Street, London WC1X 9JD

First published in the United States of America in 2026 by
Thames & Hudson Inc., 500 Fifth Avenue, New York, New York 10110

Edited and designed by Andrew Brown

EU Authorized Representative: Interart S.A.R.L.
19 rue Charles Auray, 93500 Pantin, Paris, France
productsafety@thameshudson.co.uk
interart.fr

A CIP catalogue record for this book is available from the British Library

Library of Congress Control Number 2024949595

ISBN 978-0-500-02931-2
01

Printed and bound in China by C&C Offset Printing Co. Ltd

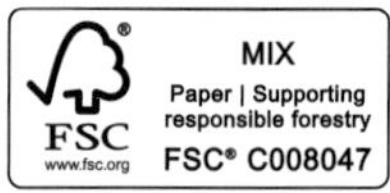

CONTENTS

INTRODUCTION

BY LOUISE ROGERS LALAURIE

'All that remains is for me to record some remarks, some notes taken over the course of my life as a painter. For which I beg of those with the patience to read them the indulgence generally granted to the writings of painters.'

In Henri Matisse's handwritten text for *Jazz* (1947), the book that introduced his extraordinary paper cut-outs to the world at large, the artist hopes that his readers will be kind. He is a painter, not a writer, and therefore accustomed to expressing himself with colours and lines, not words. And yet the words that accompany *Jazz*'s dynamic, dazzling pictures are fascinating in their own right: a heartfelt, personal creed that looks back over a life of struggle against the critics, the French art establishment, and reactionary public taste, and finds no cause for bitterness or hate, only thankfulness and serenity on the brink of old age.

Authentic self-expression in colour and line was the quest of a lifetime in Matisse's art. But while he famously advised his young students to cut out their tongues and communicate solely by the brush, his own, evocative words have come down to us in *Jazz* and other writings, and through a lifetime of letters to family and friends, sampled and presented here.

In particular, the artist's correspondence with a loyal band of classmates from art school charts his creative highs and lows, family crises, globetrotting travels, and setbacks both physical and moral: Matisse's world, captured not in paint but in writing. The early flurries of jocular, gossipy, sometimes ribald postcards and letters present a whirl of trips abroad, art dealers, patrons, and critics, followed closely by commentary and anxious, sometimes desperate requests for news through the wars of 1914–18 and 1939–45. Heartfelt advice and mature musings on art and life lead us on through the decades, to touching reminiscences and reflections in his final years.

Matisse mastered the spoken word, too, and extracts from his interviews and broadcasts are also included here. He spoke freely (too freely, he sometimes felt) to writers and journalists such as Guillaume Apollinaire, Louis Aragon, and Pierre Courthion, the last of whom conducted a series of revealing conversations in 1941. In the darkest hours of the Second World War, Matisse was visited twice by reporters from the public radio network of the Nazi-appeasing Vichy regime, in his panoramic studio in a hill-top suburb of Nice. Each time, he seized the moment to broadcast a scorching critique of the Académie des beaux-arts, the French art authority with the power to grant coveted state commissions and residencies at the Villa Médicis in Rome, which had relocated temporarily to a mansion nearby.

Often, in the decade prior to his death in 1954, Matisse's letters and interviews evoke what he called his 'second life', when his newfound serenity and sense of purpose combined with the decline in his physical powers to lead him away from painting. Today, we feel the release in his often vast cut-paper compositions – their explosive joy, pure colours, and curvaceous forms – as fiercely as when they were first made. Crowning even that achievement, Matisse spent his very last years designing the Chapel of the Rosary in Vence, in south-east France, where architecture, stained glass, graphic murals, and even the ceremonial objects and priests' vestments respond to the region's intense, clear light in a space of exceptional beauty.

As we enjoy these amazing late works, it can be all too easy to forget the strife and troubles that preceded them. Across the first half of the twentieth century, Matisse lived through two unprecedented world wars, brought vividly to life in his letters. Decades before he was denounced by the Nazis as a 'degenerate' artist, he had been dismissed by officialdom in France as a *fauve* (a 'wild beast') and a rebel. His work was praised and sought after in Russia, Britain, and the United States, but official recognition at home came much later: he was made an officer in the Légion d'honneur at the age of fifty-five, and a commander at seventy-seven. Only in 1950, at the age of eighty-one, was he selected to represent France at the Venice Biennale (where he received the Golden Lion for painting).

There were private difficulties and scandals, too. The young Henri abandoned his law studies for a bohemian existence as an art student in Paris. His daughter Marguerite was conceived with his lover Camille Joblaud, born out of wedlock, and then raised as her own by his wife Amélie, from whom he would separate at the outbreak of war in 1939, when he fled the capital for Nice in the company of Amélie's former nurse and assistant Lydia Delectorskaya. In 1944, both Amélie and Marguerite were arrested by the Gestapo, as agents of the French Resistance. Marguerite was tortured but somehow recovered, to the astonishment of her doctors, despite the long shadow cast by an earlier trauma, when Matisse himself had been forced to assist in an emergency tracheotomy performed on her as child.

Through it all, Matisse worked and worked tirelessly, pursuing hard-won authenticity of expression like a 'mindless brute kicking a door'. Plagued by insomnia and debilitating pain, he underwent life-saving surgery in 1941, which left him frequently bedridden though also, in his own words, 'reborn'. When he was too incapacitated to paint, or exhausted by a long day at the easel, he would work at a bedtable, rehearsing his free-flowing, gestural drawing technique over and over again, and illuminating the poetry of French greats such as the Renaissance master Pierre de Ronsard, the Symbolist Stéphane Mallarmé, and the *flâneur* and *poète maudit* Charles Baudelaire.

Matisse loved to craft books in which words and pictures work together on the page, generating new meanings of their own. It is a legacy honoured here as we pair his own words and pictures to chart the long, eventful life of this defining master of twentieth-century art – the distance travelled, and the lessons learned.

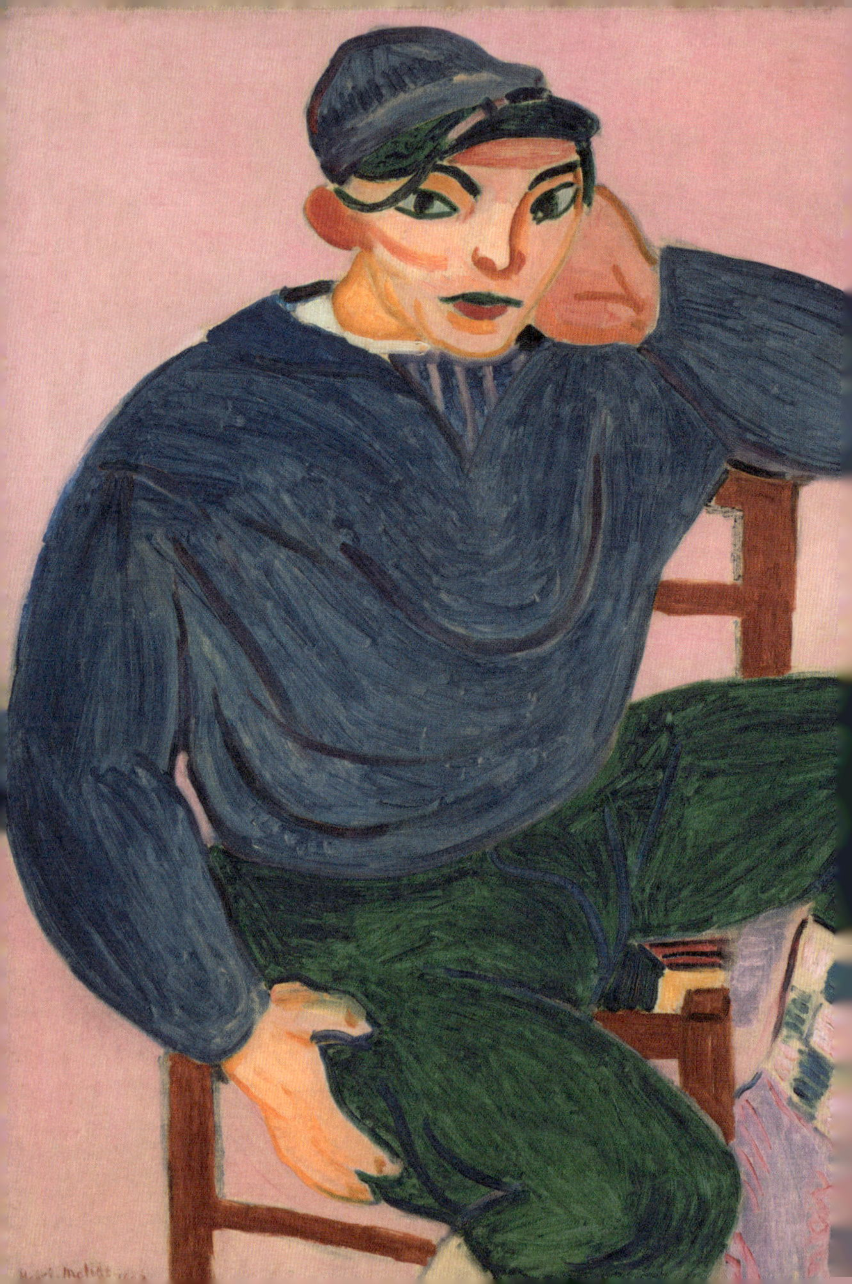

YOUTH

There were no painters in my family, no painters where I came from.

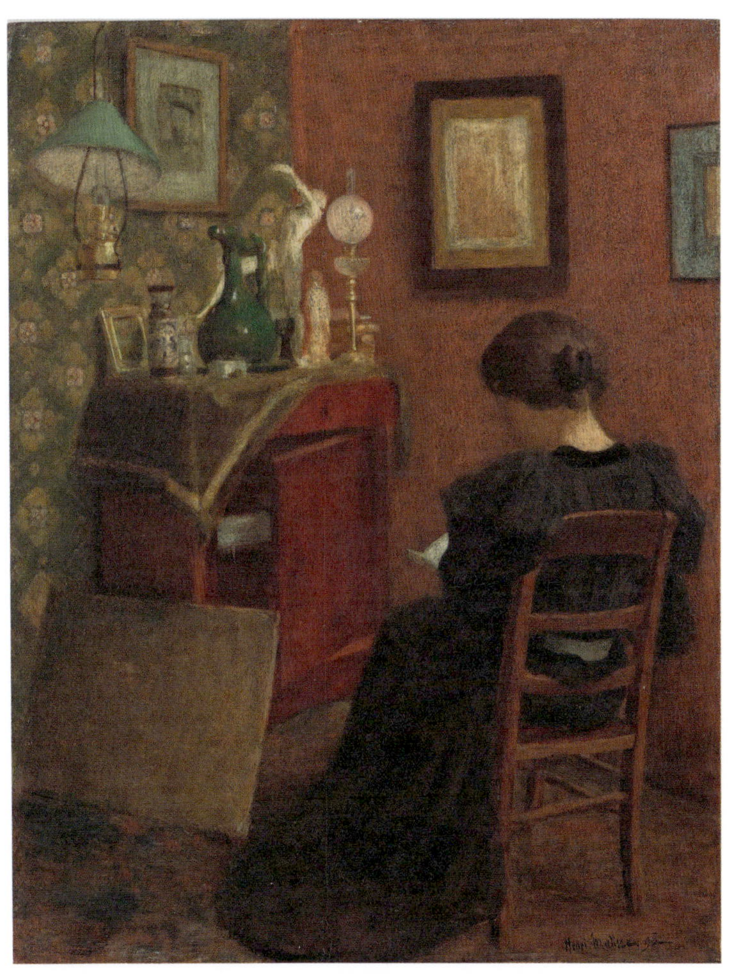

Woman Reading, 1895. Oil on canvas, 61.5 × 48 cm (24¼ × 18⅞ in.).

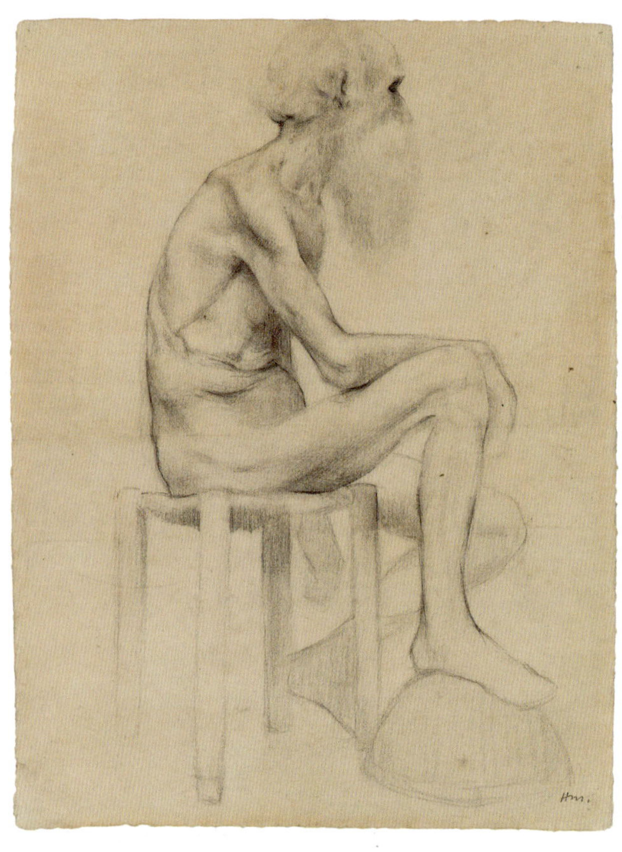

Study of Seated Old Man, Paris, *c.* 1893–5.
Charcoal on watermarked Canson laid paper,
63 × 48 cm (24⅞ × 19 in.).

Before painting, I was perpetually anxious, irritated, bored, by the different things people would have me do.

Quite by chance, I took drawing classes with my friend.... We were the most attentive pupils, scratching away at our paper, scrutinizing the model ... a cast of fig leaves, or a Roman bust.

Drawing came easily to me, with no idea at all of taking it further in any way.... I had chronic appendicitis. I had time on my hands, and I filled it.

And then I got my paints, my colours. I was twenty-one.... The moment I held the box of colours in my hands, I sensed that here was my life. Like an animal turning naturally to the things it loves.

That was the seed, the kernel ... the bud that was destined to burst.

Nothing interested me before, but then painting was all I could think about. Like a weed shooting up out of nowhere.

I felt powerfully drawn to painting, a sort of Paradise Found where I was totally free, alone, at peace.

My father had paid for my law studies. When I said, 'I want to be a painter', it was like telling him, 'What you have done is pointless.'

'When will the negligent Henri Matisse deign to reply to his parents?', my father would write.

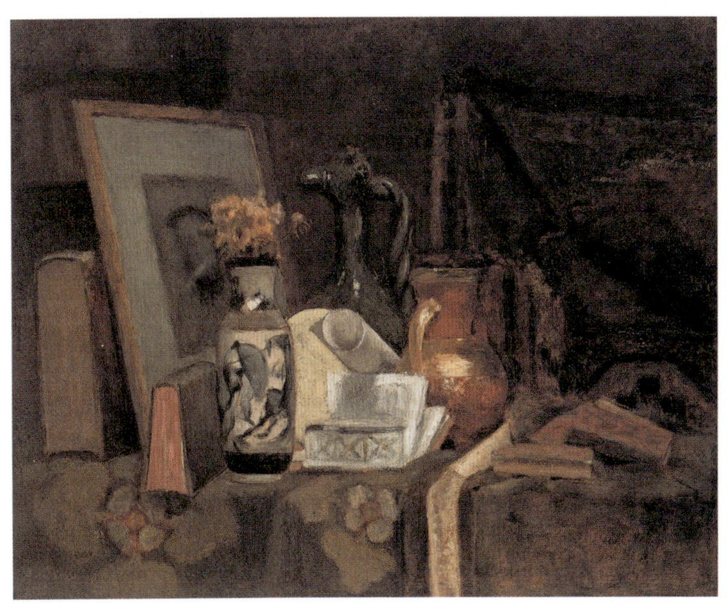

Still Life with Self-Portrait, 1896.
Oil on canvas, 64.8 × 81.2 cm (25¼ × 32 in.).

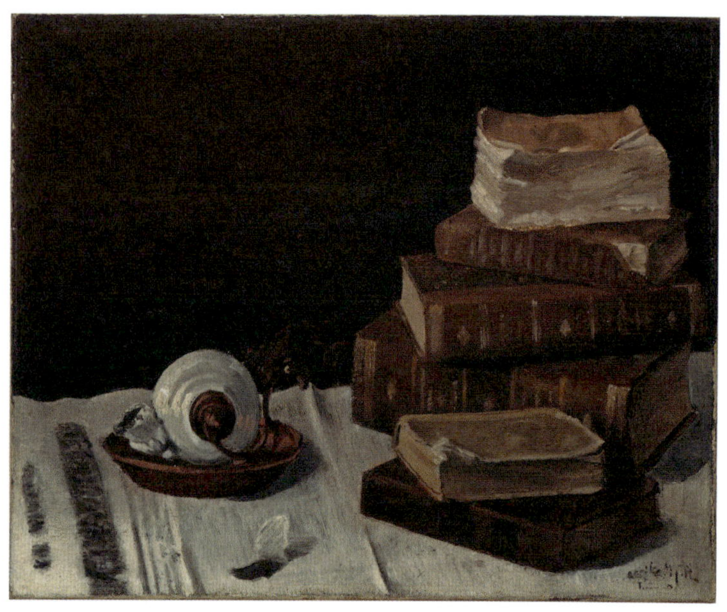

Still Life with Books, 1890.
Oil on canvas, 21.5 × 27 cm (8½ × 10¾ in.).

In my parents' attic,
I found the first painting
I ever did: my first still
life ... with my law books.
I was surprised to see
in that canvas everything
that I had done since.

For a young painter, life is hard: if he is sincere ... absorbed in his research, he will be incapable of painting to please the art-loving public.

❧

If a young painter ... works only to please and sell, he loses the bedrock of his own conscience and depends on the whims of others, neglecting and ultimately losing his gifts.

❧

I should like to live long enough to revisit my youthful world view and see what my new work would add to it.

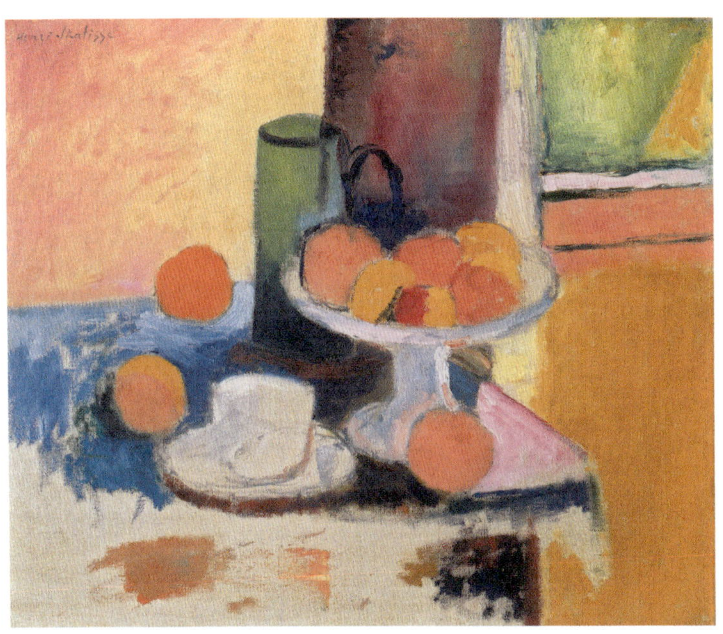

Still Life with Oranges, 1899.
Oil on canvas, 46.7 × 55.2 cm (18⅜ × 21¾ in.).

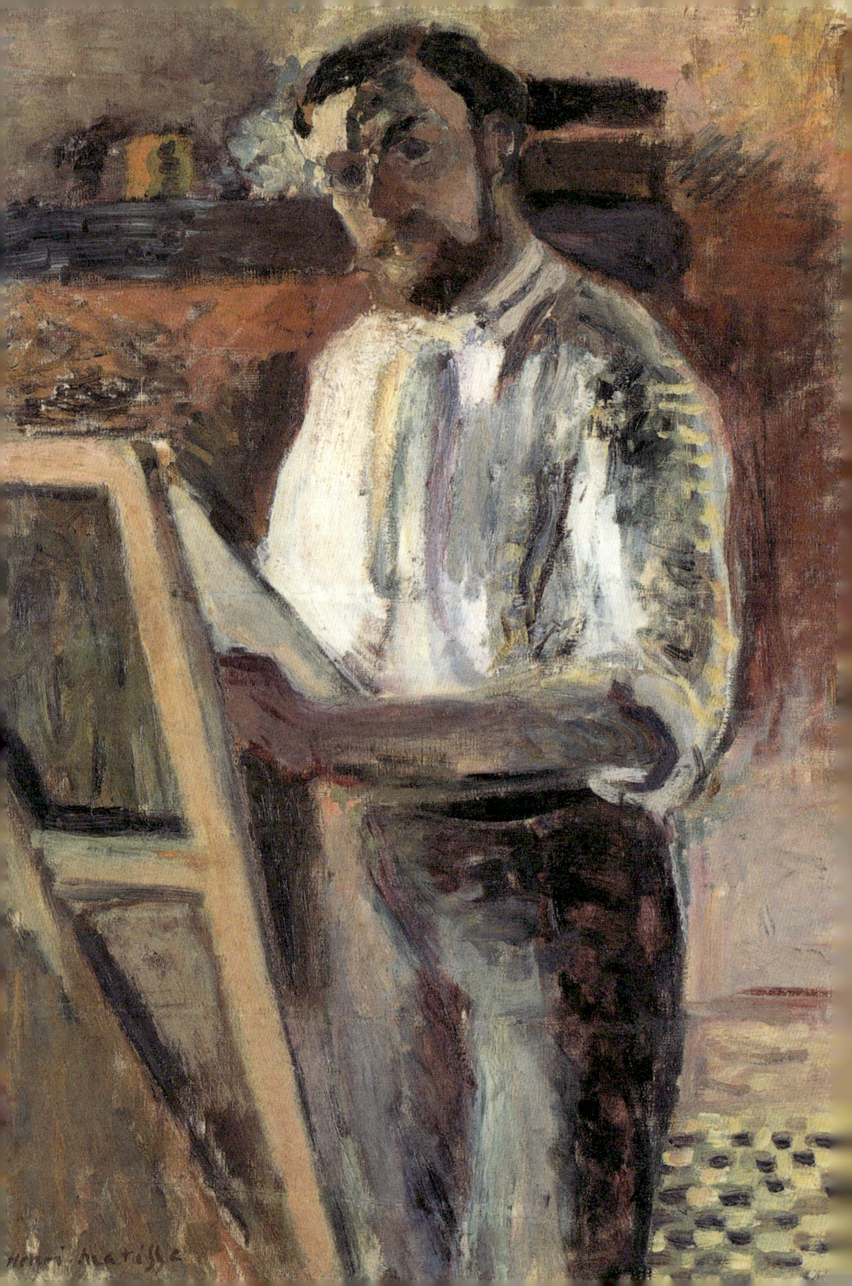
Henri Matisse

WORK AND INSPIRATION

Find joy in the sky, in the trees, in flowers. There are flowers everywhere, for those who truly wish to see them.

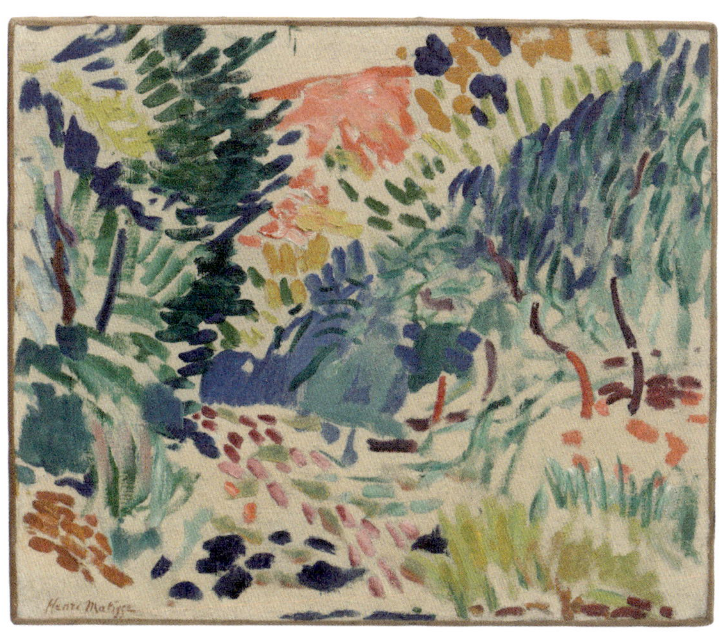

Landscape at Collioure, 1905. Oil on canvas, 38.8 × 46.6 cm (15¼ × 18⅜ in.).

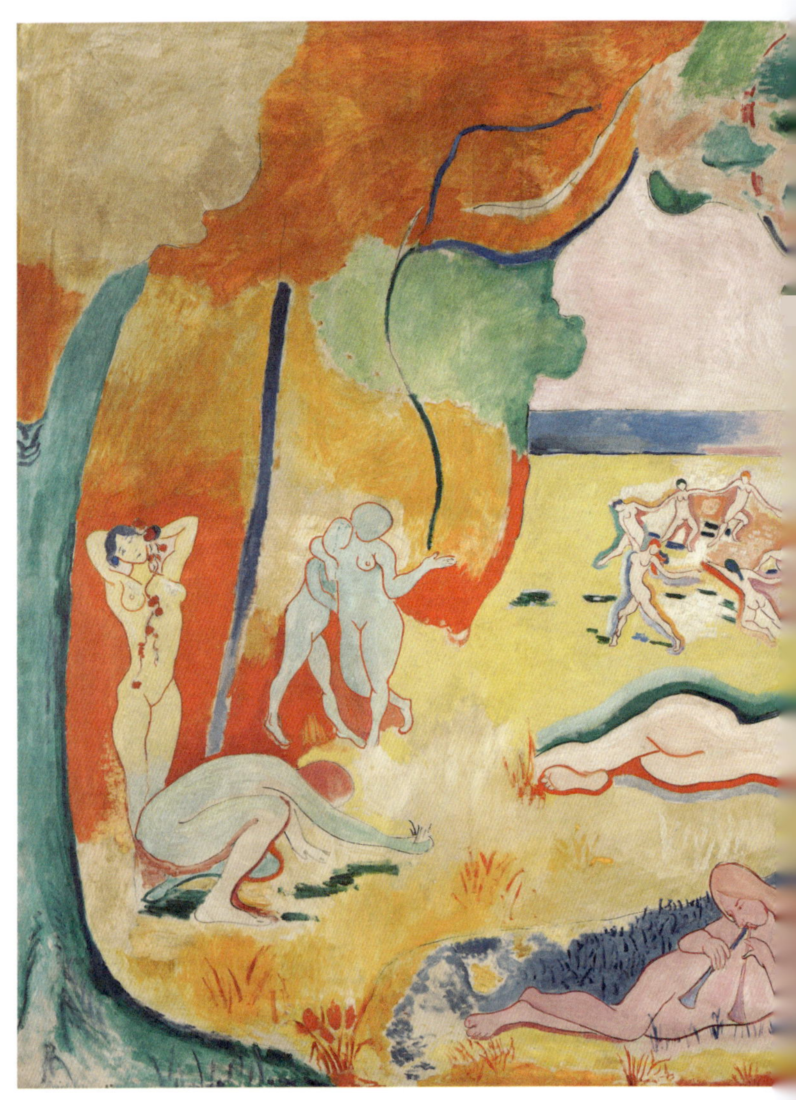

Le Bonheur de vivre (The Joy of Life), 1905–6.
Oil on canvas, 176.5 × 240.7 cm (69½ × 94¾ in.).

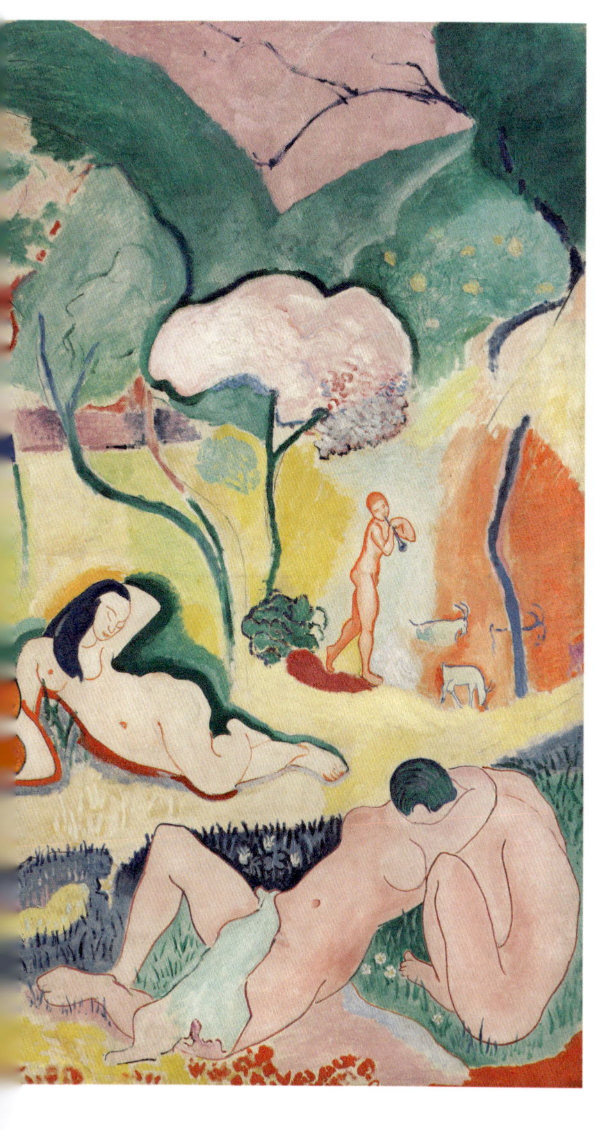

I took a walk beside the Seine, to the bird market. I was surprised by the colours. Straightaway, I wanted to buy them, as always when something catches me by surprise.... I bought a green one, a blue one, a yellow one.

We slept in Agay.... Porphyry rocks dotted with small, bright green pine trees ... the sea, blue, like indigo dye ... fringed with spray ... a delicate greenish-white against the red ... made sublime in the setting sun.

Every day I see the sun rise, at 5 a.m., colouring Nice and its mountains.

The sun rises behind me. I see the mountains towards Cagnes colour up first, then the castle in Nice, and finally the city, every day at 5 a.m. See how diligent I am!

I am not really a traveller. I am a sedentary worker who starts his day on time each morning, finishes at noon, then starts again ... and works on until the evening.

I have been working ... in full sunlight from 10 a.m. to midday, and I am worn out for the rest of the day.

I am a workhorse. Two sittings a day, every day, except Friday afternoon.... Am I happy? No, precisely because I am working so hard.

Galley slaves that we are, with none of the security that makes for a good night's sleep.

I am working tremendously hard all day, with great passion, because it is the only true and certain thing there is.

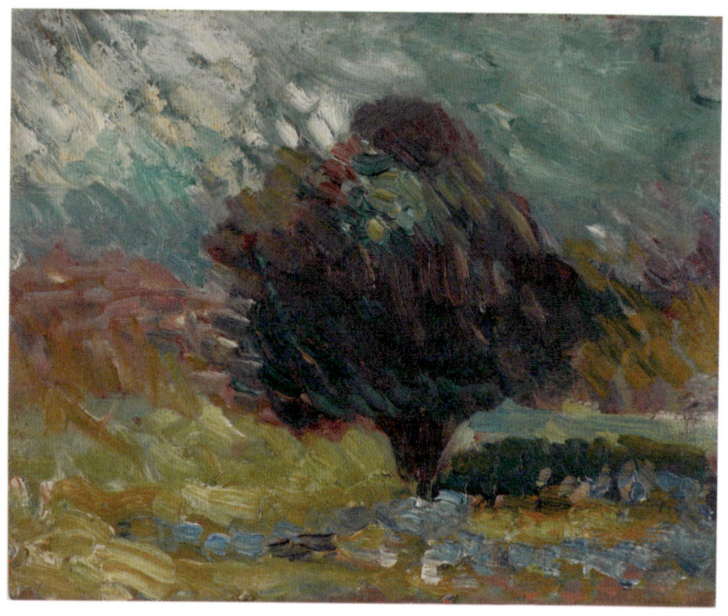

The Tree, 1898. Oil on cardboard, 16.5 × 20.3 cm (6½ × 8 in.).

Starting tomorrow, I begin at 6.30 a.m. or 7 a.m. The olive trees are so beautiful at that hour.

The full midday sun is superb but terrifying.

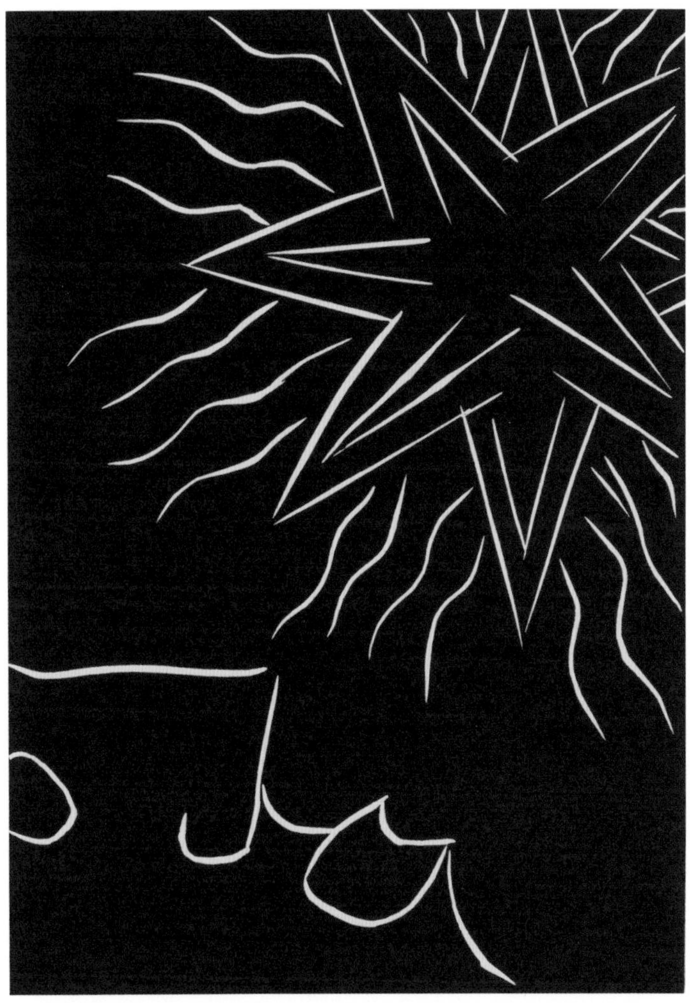

'But suddenly the sun, shaking its mane', from *Pasiphaé: Chant de Minos (Les Crétois)*, 1944. Linoleum cut from book, 32 × 24.8 cm (12⅝ × 9¾ in.).

To get the day off to a good start, I need to feel murderous ... as if I have something to give, energy to expend. When you feel that way, off you go.

The artist must bring all his energy, his sincerity, and the greatest modesty to his work.

Work a few hours each day, apply yourself to the task, and, have no doubt, you will make a life in the moment, relieved of your burdens.

Just paint, a few hours each day, to lift the weight of our current difficulties and concerns from your shoulders.

Find happiness in yourself, in a good day's work, the light it can bring to the fog all around.

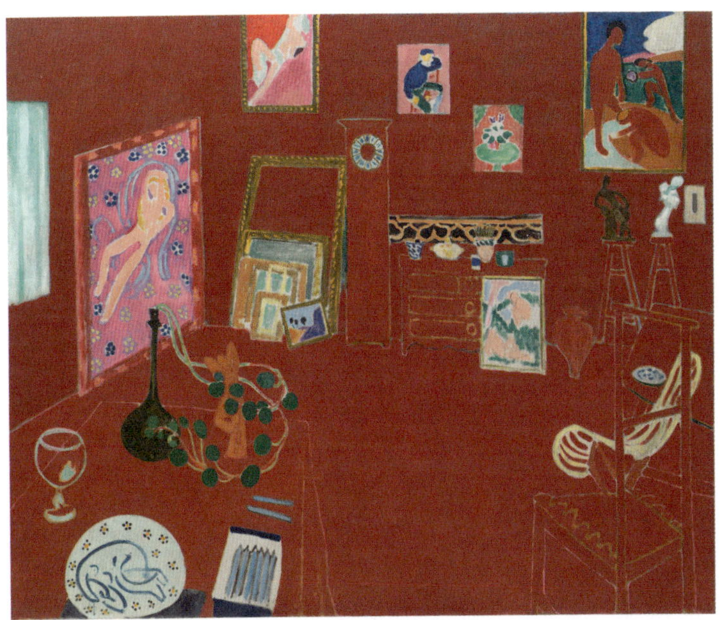

The Red Studio, 1911. Oil on canvas, 181 × 219.1 cm (71¼ × 86¼ in.).

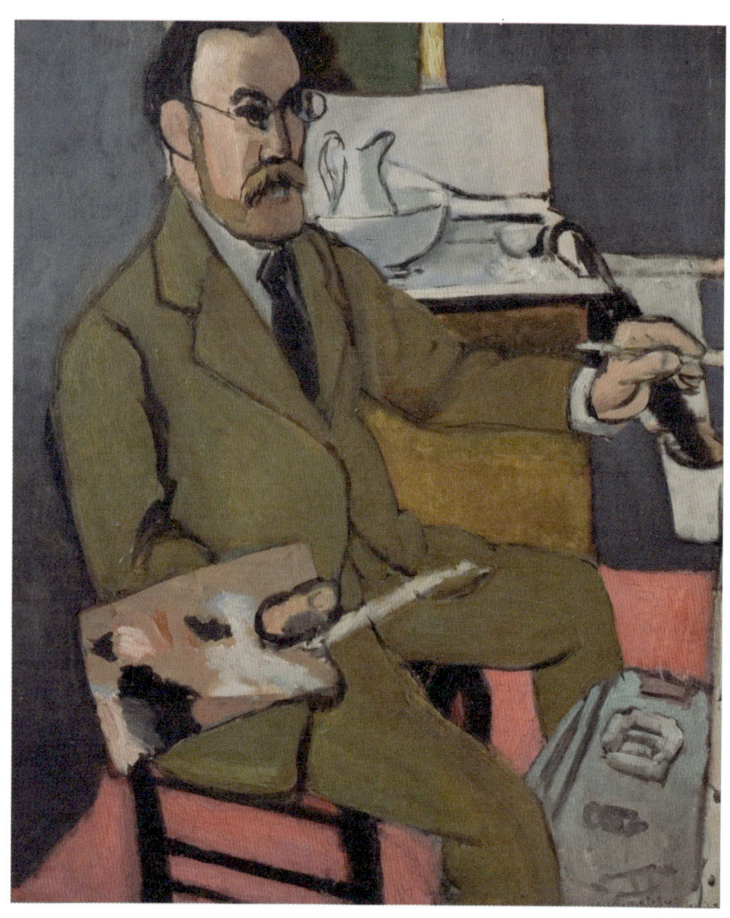

Self-Portrait, 1918. Oil on canvas,
65 × 54 cm (25½ × 21¼ in.).

An artist is only in full possession of his faculties and in his right mind when he is in front of his easel.

I need the unexpected.... Renoir told me, 'I spend time arranging a bouquet of flowers, and when I think I have finished ... it is the unseen, unintended side that I paint.'

Cast aside the old clichés, that come so readily to hand and may stifle the little flower that never shows itself where we expect.

Method is essential, but genius is the untamed shoot that bursts out from the hedge.

When I have a moment to spare, the ideas never come. You know how it is.

Your letter finds me prostrate, utterly discouraged ... paralysed by some conventionality I cannot pin down, that prevents me from expressing myself in painting as I would wish.

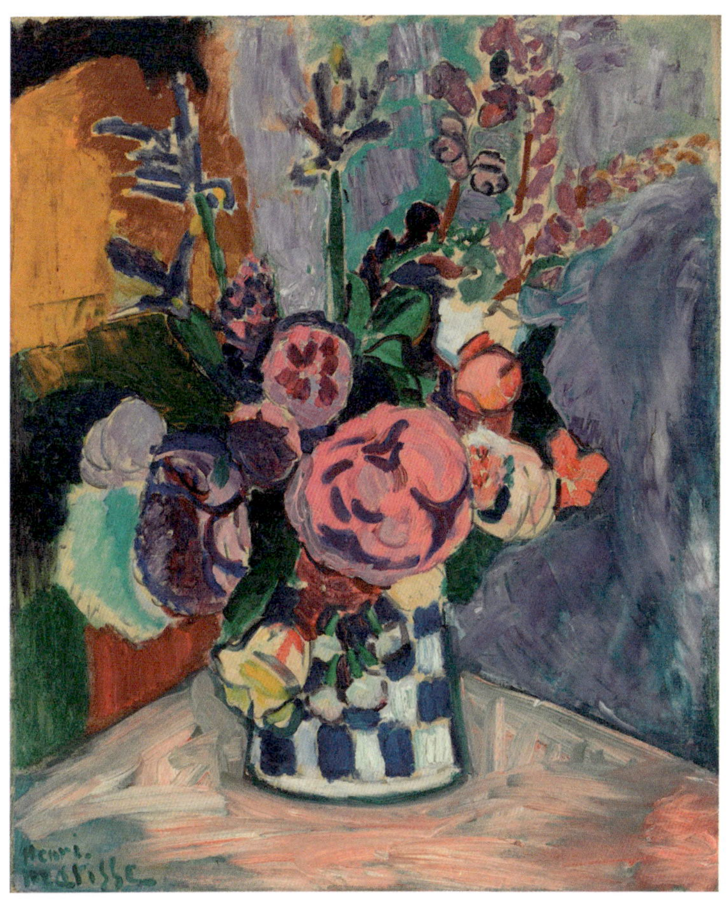

Les Pivoines, 1907. Oil on canvas,
65 × 54.6 cm (25½ × 21½ in.).

Looking back, my whole life has been this way. A moment of despair, followed by a brief, joyous moment of revelation that allows me to do something unfeasibly brilliant - and that itself leaves me lost, disorientated at the prospect of the next new thing.

When I thought I had finished and put the tops back on my colours, I took my canvas home and have left it facing the wall ever since, for fear of disappointment.

I never release a painting or a drawing without first giving it all my effort. And if, after that, I still feel I can let it live, then I am quietly confident of the path it will trace for me, in the mind and spirit of anyone who sees it.

I had a visit from Madame [Gertrude] Stein.... She sorted out my painting, good and proper, took it to pieces ... with great authority ... but after she left, I saw that my picture was really very good.

I have never avoided the influence of others. I would have seen that as cowardly, a failure to be honest with myself.

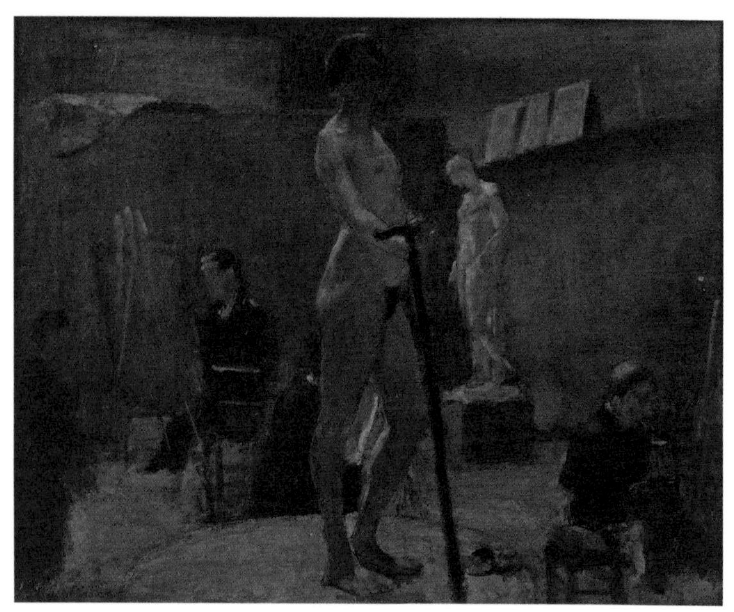

Gustave Moreau's Studio, 1895. Oil on canvas,
65 × 81 cm (25⅝ × 31⅞ in.).

Only one teacher counted for me: Gustave Moreau, who had many pupils, from whom he produced a handful of authentic artists.

Moreau's great quality was not to push a pupil to satisfy the requirements of a series of academic tests, but to see that the development of their mind is continuous, lifelong.

Since the earliest times (from cave carvings to modern painters), artists have enriched our shared visual vocabulary.

Each new generation looks through the eyes of artists from the generation before.

Behind us, we must keep everything we have learned, and still retain the freshness of instinct.

When I see Giotto's frescoes in Padua ... straightaway, I understand the sentiment expressed, because it's there in the lines, in the composition, in the colour.

Giotto is the pinnacle ... but nowadays, the path to an equivalent is too long for one life. Still, the staging posts are interesting, along the way.

Rembrandt ... is always noble. That is a word I can never say when I look at a painting by Delacroix, which is strange, and a little disappointing.

I have become glued to a woman. I spend all my time with her.... Fortunately, the woman is made of plaster and her name is Night, by Michelangelo.

I hope to make Michelangelo's clarity and complexity of structure my own.

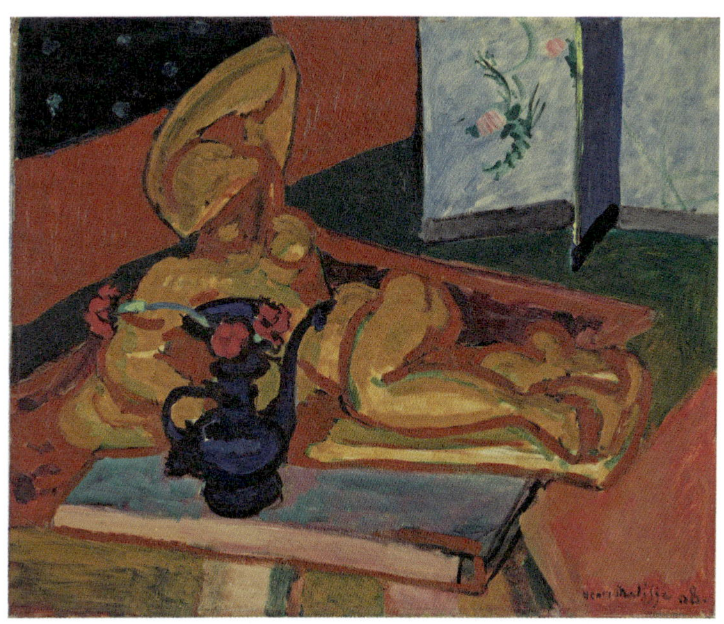

The Bronze Figure, 1908. Oil on canvas, 60.5 × 73 cm (23⅞ × 29 in.).

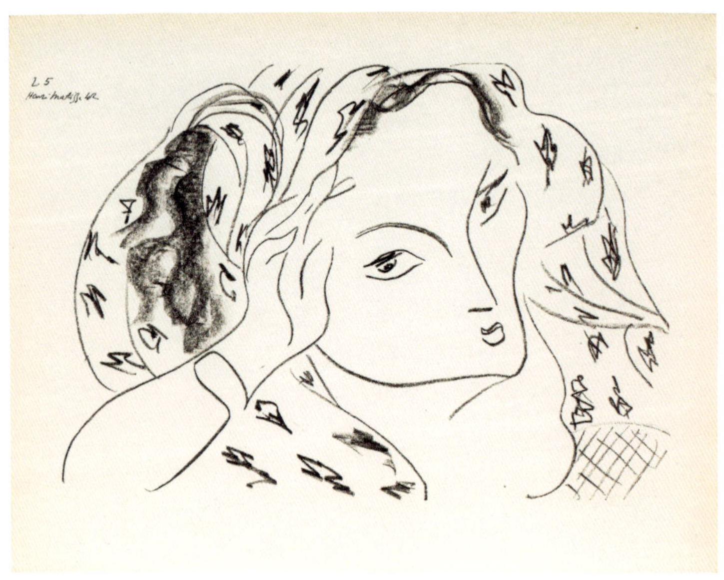

Theme L, variation 5, from *Dessins: Thèmes et Variations*, 1943. Linocut, lithograph, and reproductions on Japan impérial and Vélin d'Arches paper, 33.5 × 25.3 cm (13¼ × 10 in.).

Those Burmese statues ... a little like the arms I do ... ending in a hand like a flower at the tip of a stem.

There are two types of artist, the ones who do a portrait of a hand ... a new hand every time ... while others do the sign for a hand, like Delacroix. With signs you can create free, ornamental compositions.

Other artists have invented their own signs, but to copy them is to copy a dead thing: their emotional destination, not your own.

I must create ... the sign for a tree. And not ... as it has existed before, with other artists.

An artist's importance is measured in the number of new signs they bring to the visual vocabulary.

I am like a seaplane.... Once airborne [the floaters] are forgotten ... [but] the floaters are ... the Louvre ... the Old Masters ... all the things that I have known.

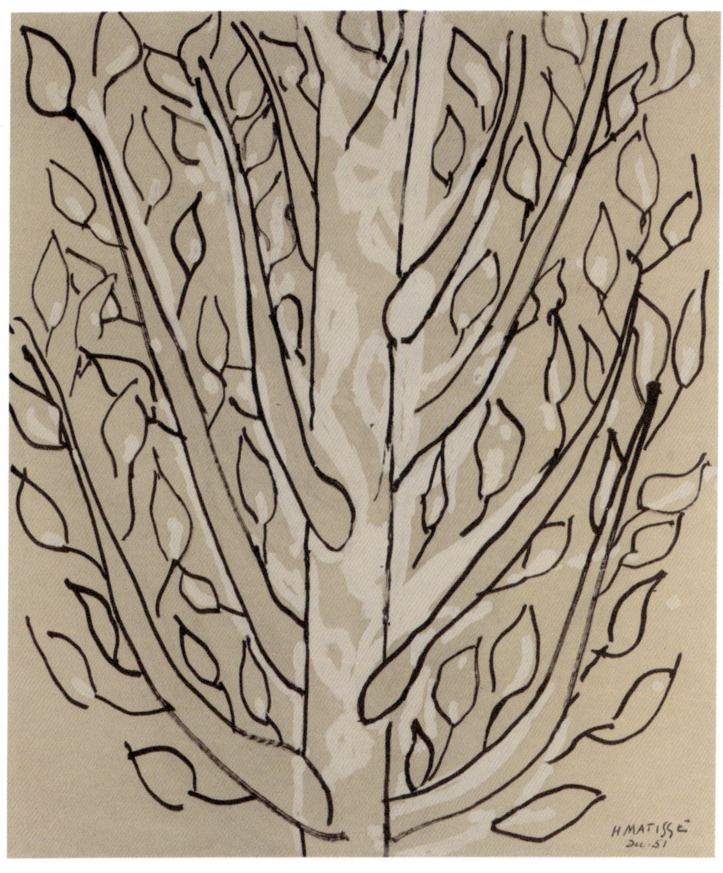

The Tree, 1951. Brush and black ink, white gouache, and charcoal on tan paper mounted on canvas, 177.8 × 152.4 cm (70 × 60 in.).

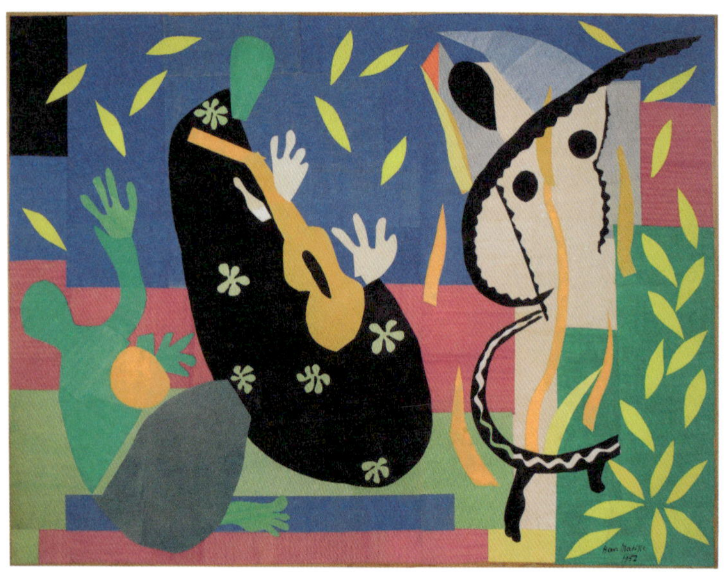

The Sorrow of the King, 1952. Gouache on paper on canvas, 292 × 386 cm (115 × 152 in.).

I worked non-stop for fifty years, head down.... The result was a body of work that has some influence. Happily. Otherwise, I would be completely useless.

We have ... our contradictions. And from these we must craft ... something permanent.... It is what drives us to work to the very end, if we haven't run away, lost interest, become mired in routine.

I hope I will find a few more years of decent work, so that I can end my life's labour with paintings that will clearly show what it is I have been trying to say.... There will be no point in working after that.

It was the hope of still progressing in his work that kept Renoir alive.

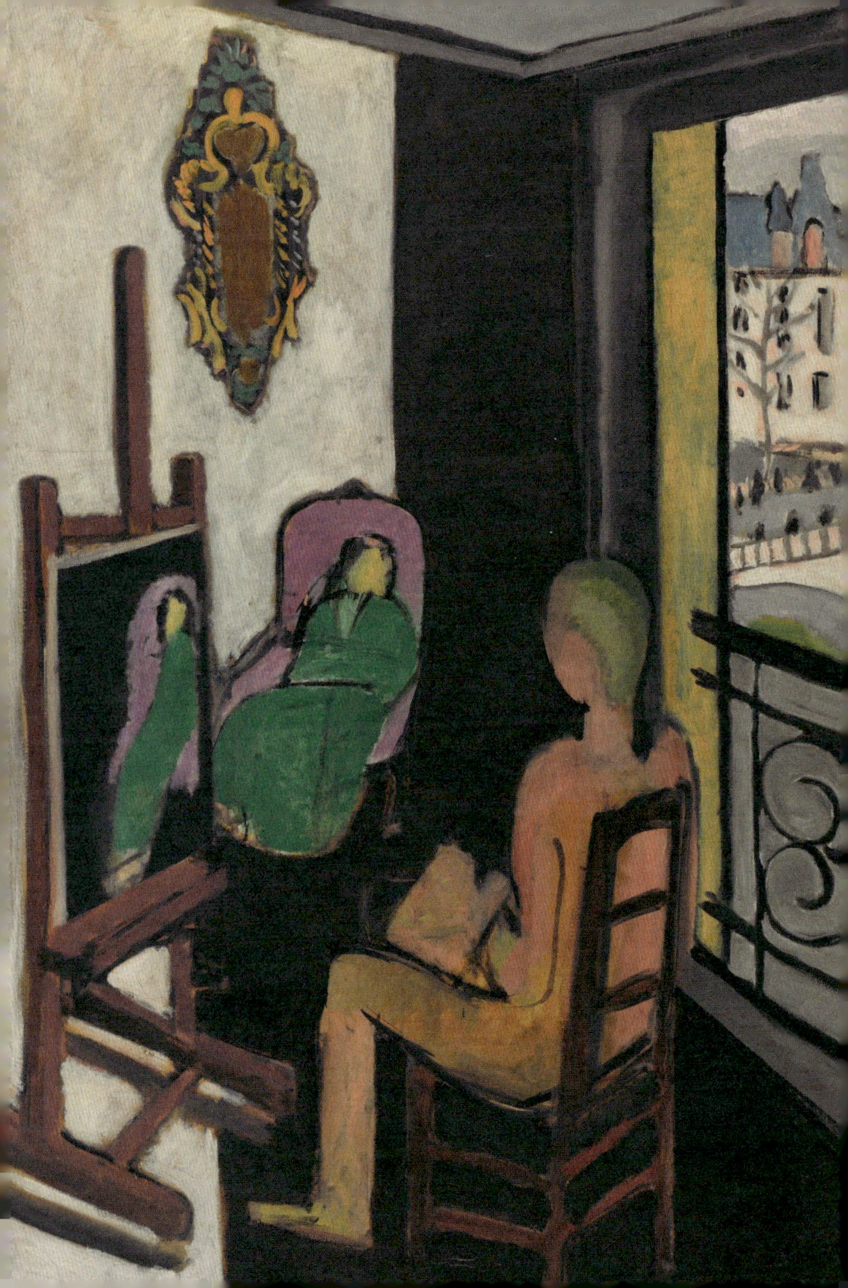

MAKING ART

I have found a way of drawing that, after some preliminary work, allows me to convey everything I feel.

❧

I trust my hand to draw because while I was training it ... I tried hard never to let it get ahead of my feelings.

❧

The hand is merely the extension of the artist's sensibility and intelligence. The more supple it is, the more obedient. The servant must never become the master.

❧

You do not deliver a slap limply, indecisively.... [I draw] with a firm, untrembling hand.

❧

I showed my drawings to Rodin. He said, 'You have an easy, draughtsman's hand. Beware of that.'

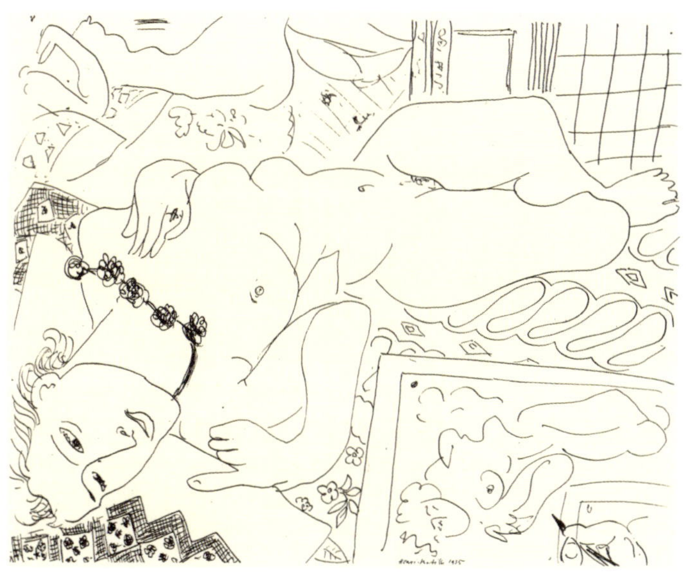

Nude Lying Down, 1935. Pen and India ink on paper, 45 × 57 cm (17¾ × 22½ in.).

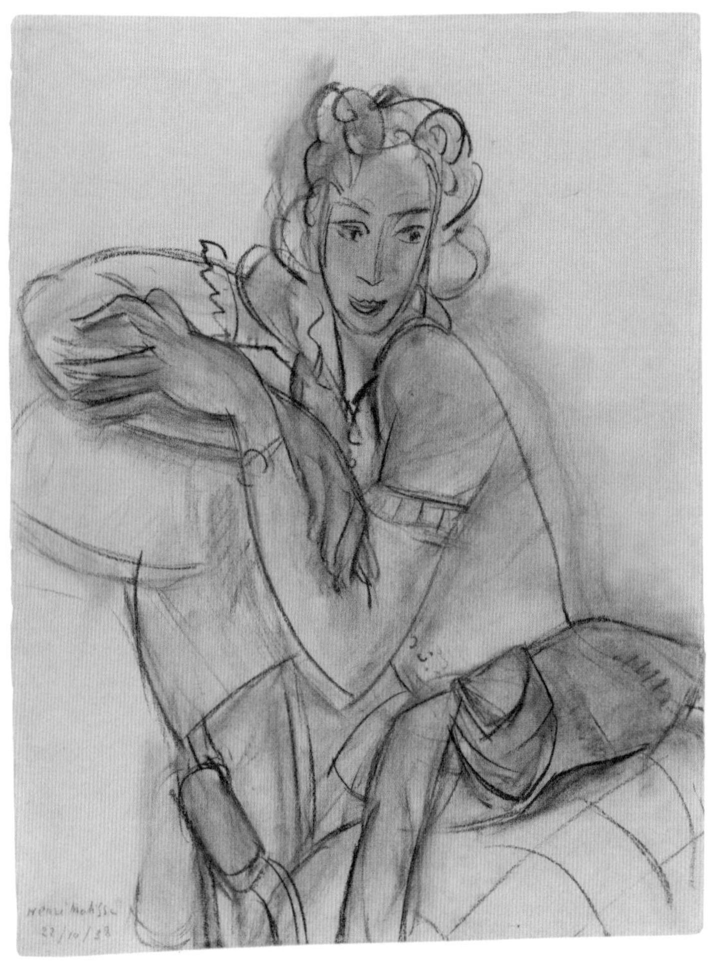

Study for 'The Song', Portrait of Hélène Mercier, née Princess Galitzine, Seated, 1938. Charcoal and stump on paper, 65.5 × 50.5 cm (25¾ × 19⅞ in.).

The drawing appears before me as if each charcoal line had been drawn on a mirror, in the condensation that has prevented me from seeing it until now.

My use of the plumbline always serves me well.
The vertical axis is in my soul.... I never mark a curve ...
without knowing its relationship to the vertical.
My curves are not mad.

The white of the canvas shines through the layer of applied colour. But apply a second layer, and that vibrancy is extinguished.... You have to start all over again, courageously, to triumph over the medium, with a few expressive colour values.

I am sure that these paintings - vivid as they are - can be done only in oils, whereas previously ... I thought only in terms of line and colour, and the medium - watercolours, gouache - was unimportant.

There - a painting that has taken a year. Those who see only the way I have done the hair and the embroidery on the shoulder will think I am joking.

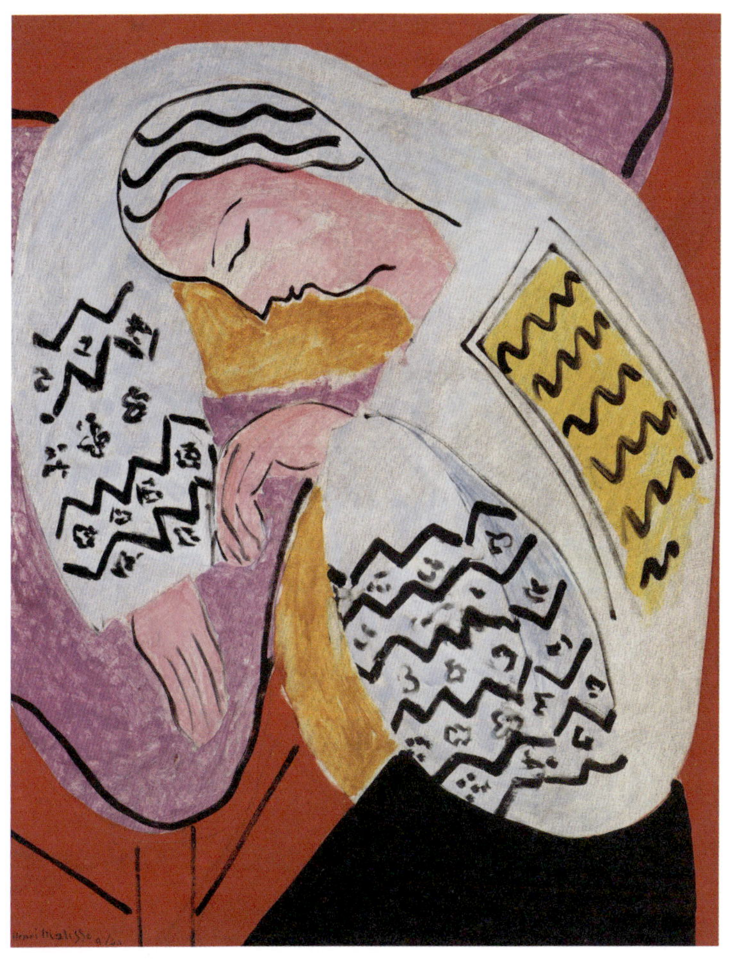

The Dream, 1940.
Oil on canvas, 81 × 65 cm (31⅞ × 25⅝ in.).

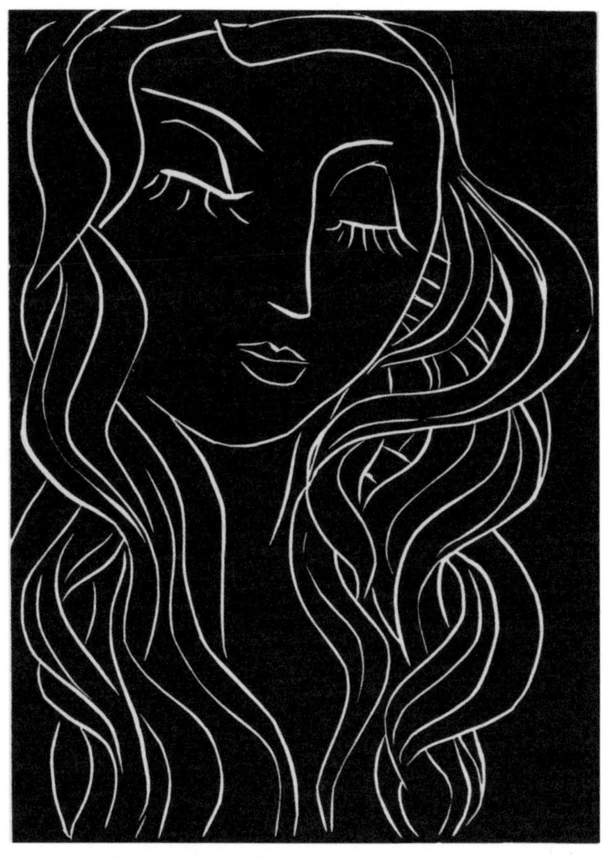

Sleep, Sleeper with the Long Eyelashes..., from *Pasiphaé: Chant de Minos (Les Crétois)*, 1943–4. Linoleum cut from book, 32 × 24.8 cm (12⅝ × 9¾ in.).

Linoleum is easy to cut ... but it demands unbroken concentration. The slightest distraction and the hand relaxes, the cutter slips, the line thins, or you press harder, unawares ... thickening the line.... The black and brilliant white are lovely, crystalline, frosty, diamantine.

Lino cutting: the gouge is like a violin bow ... directly responsive to the printmaker's sensibility.

I spent the afternoon making new colour combinations with the cut-out paper system.

Drawing with scissors: cutting directly into the living colour reminds me of free carving, as sculptors do.

Colours can change in relationship to one another: a black will become red-black against a cold colour like Prussian blue, but blue-black against [...] a warm shade of orange.

Once I have found my tonal relationships, the result should be a chord of living colours, a harmony comparable to a musical composition.

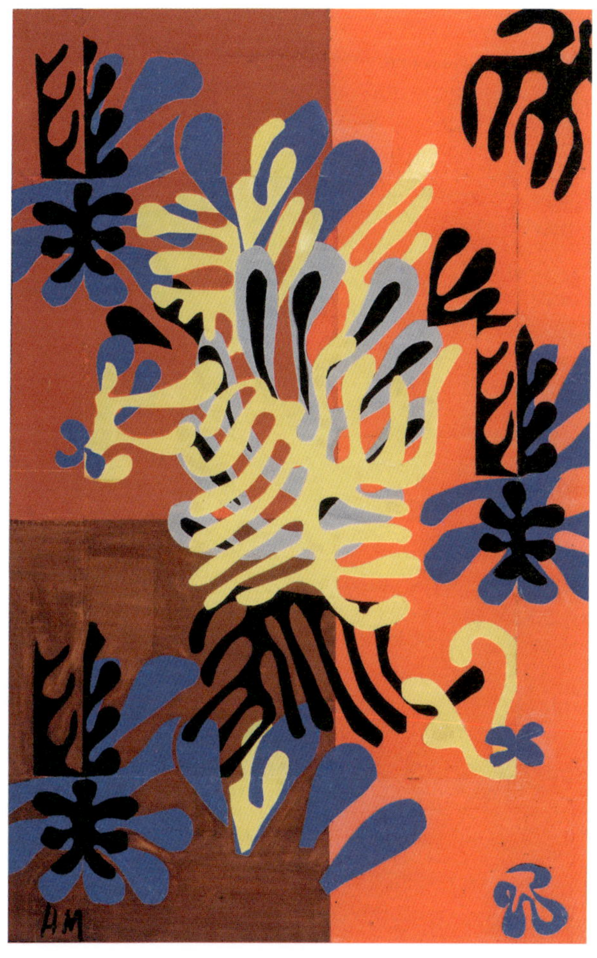

Mimosa, 1949–51. Gouache on paper, cut and pasted, mounted on canvas, 148 × 98 cm (58½ × 38⅝ in.).

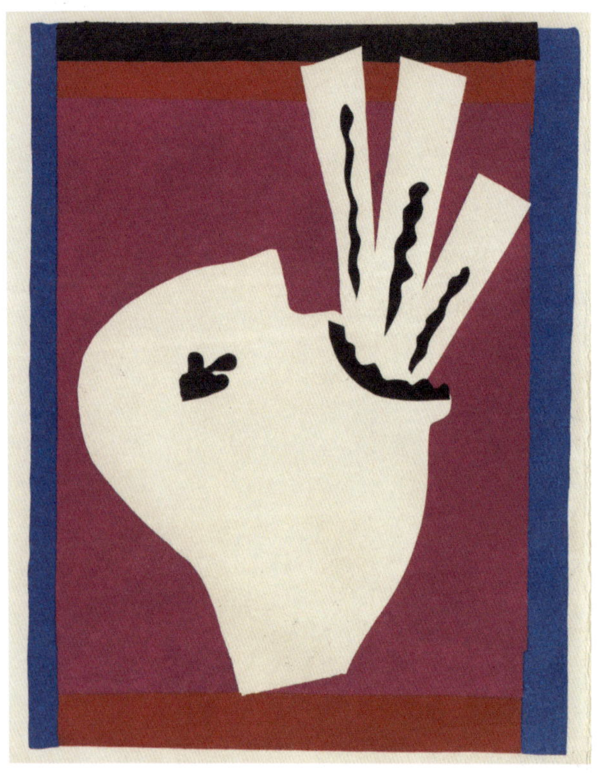

The Sword Swallower from *Jazz*, 1947. Pochoir print on paper, 39.1 × 30.3 cm (15⅜ × 11⅞ in.).

I have colours, a canvas, and I must express myself ... by placing ... four or five patches of colour, and by drawing four or five visually expressive lines.

The difficult task at hand is to achieve harmony between my drawing, my colours, and my emotions.

I would tell my young pupils, 'So you want to paint? First you must cut out your tongue: your urge removes the right to self-expression by any means but the brush.'

The only painters we truly need are those with the gift of translating their most intimate feelings into colour and drawing.

I paint to translate my sensibility – the emotions, feelings, and reactions that I experience – through colour and the drawn line.

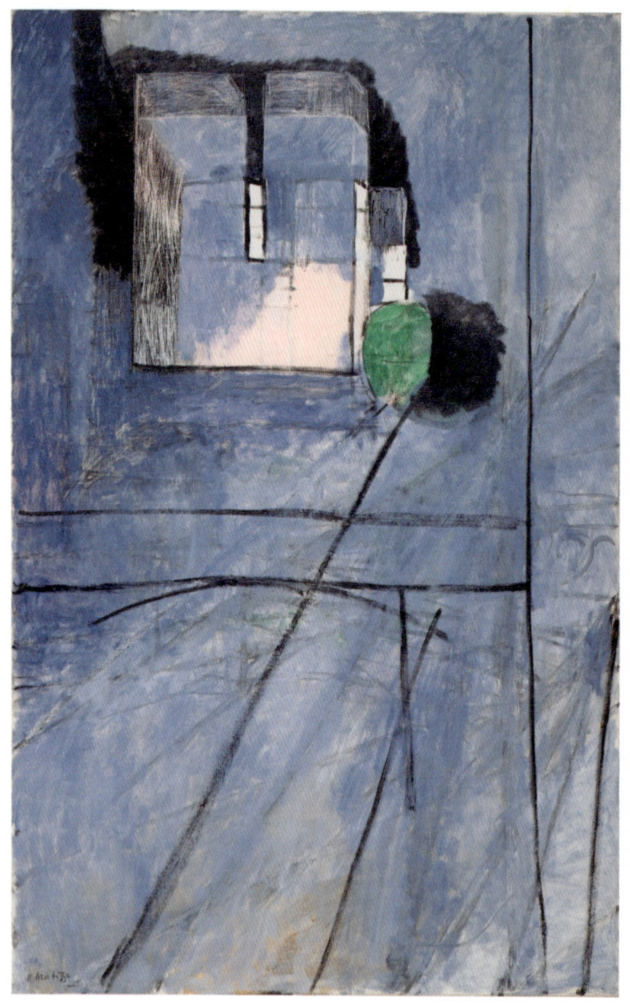

View of Notre-Dame, 1914. Oil on canvas, 147.3 × 94.3 cm (58 × 37⅛ in.).

When I put down a green, it does not mean 'grass'. When I put down a blue, it does not mean the sky.

A drawing should have an expansive energy, a force, that animates everything around it.

On a fig tree, no leaf is the same as any other … and yet each shouts 'fig'.

The point is not to draw the tree as I see it … but as an object that affects my spirit … in relation to other feelings of all kinds … which cannot be expressed through an exact copy … only once I see myself in the tree.

A new painting should be something unique, a birth that brings a new motif to the depiction of the world through the human spirit.

The most technically advanced camera cannot do what painting does – even in colour. Nor can film.

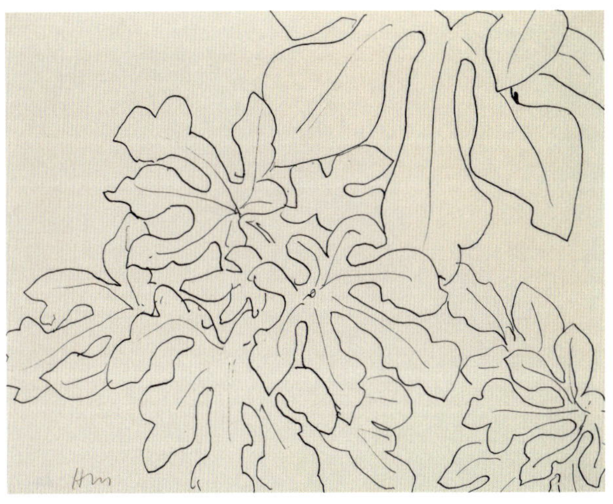

Fig Leaves (Feuilles de figuier), 1941. Pen and India ink on paper, 20.3 × 26.3 cm (8 × 10⅜ in.).

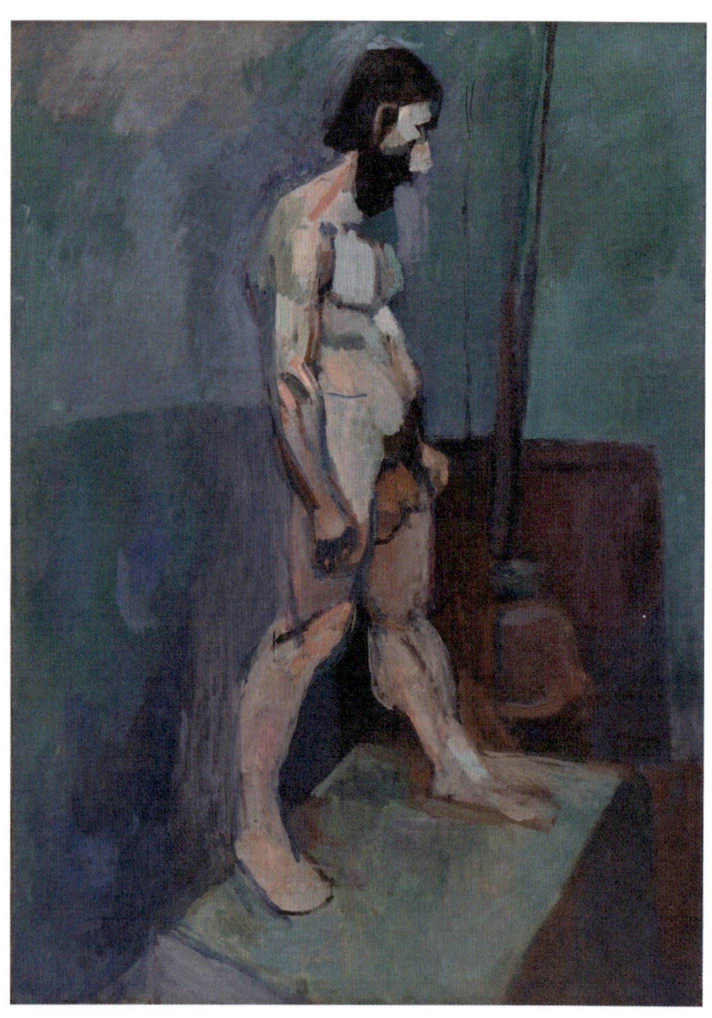

Male Model, c. 1900. Oil on canvas, 99.3 × 72.7 cm (39⅛ × 28⅝ in.).

Drawing is female,
painting is male.

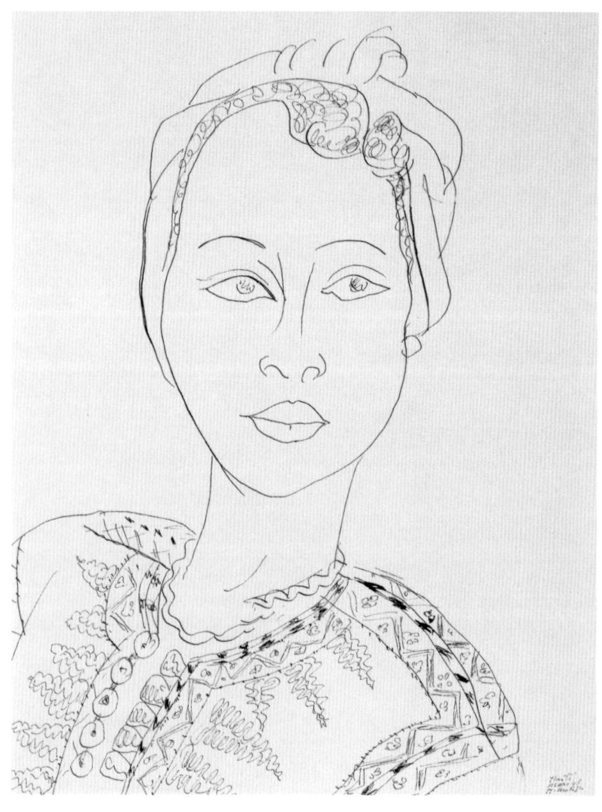

Woman with Turban (Carmen Lahens), 1943. Pen and ink on wove paper, 52.3 × 40.5 cm (20⅝ × 15⅞ in.).

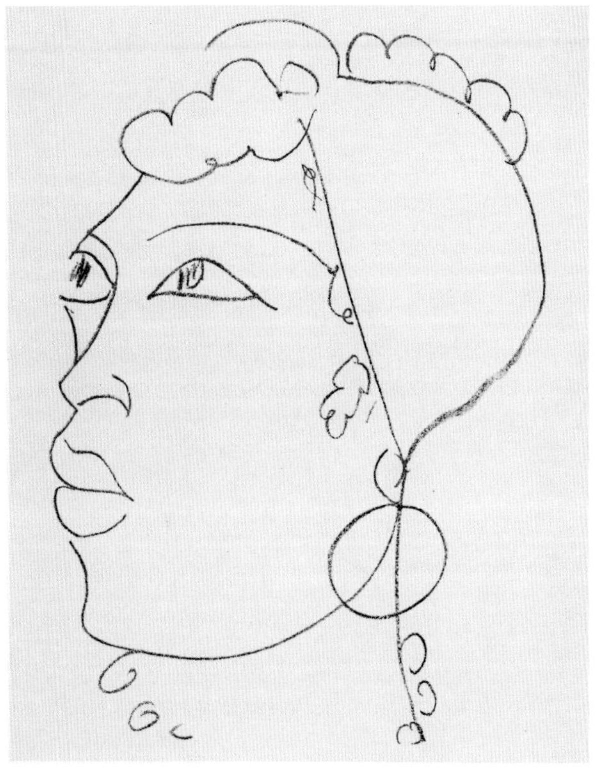

'But, not satiated', from *The Flowers of Evil*, 1947.
Etching, woodcut, and photolithograph on Rives paper, 28.6 × 23 cm (11¼ × 9⅛ in.).

Two drawings of the same face may show the same character, though the proportions ... are different.

The character of a drawn face does not depend on its different proportions, but on the spiritual light it reflects.

The ear adds enormously to the character ... it is very important to express it carefully and fully, not to suggest it with a dab.

What interests me most is ... the face.... I find the essential lines ... those that translate the high seriousness of character in every human being.

When I have a model, first I do a literal, almost photographic portrait, to immerse myself in their personality. After that, I let my hand work freely, once I feel contact has been made.

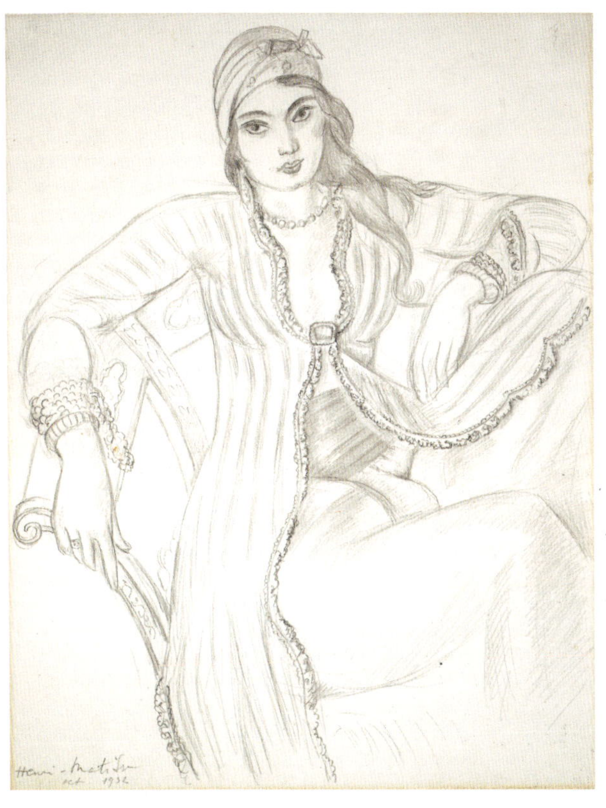

La Robe lamée, 1932. Pencil on paper, 32.4 × 25.4 cm (12¾ × 10 in.).

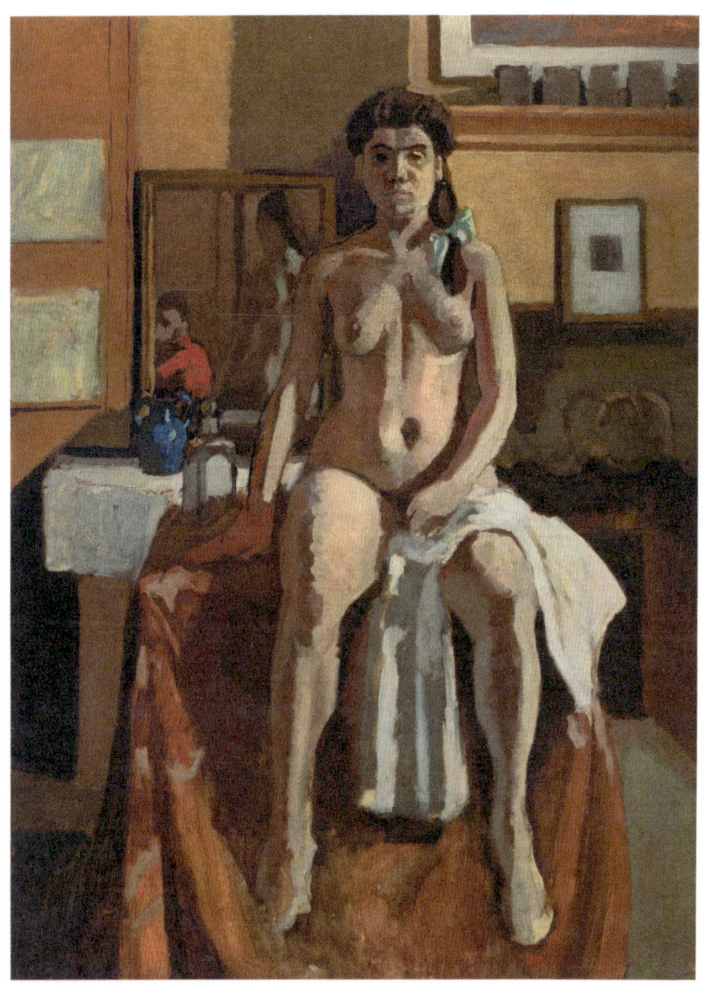

Carmelina, 1903. Oil on canvas, 81.3 × 59 cm (32 × 23¼ in.).

For others, the model is a source of information. For me, it is the thing that stops me in my tracks.

The model is the furnace that fuels my energy.

I remember Renoir telling me, 'If you knew, old friend, how I have loved womankind – and not like a lascivious boar!'

Why, if my sense of freshness, beauty, youth – in flowers, a beautiful sky, an elegant tree – is the same now as thirty years ago, should I temper it when I look at a young woman I can no longer hold?

Each time the model rested, I rested and stared absently, as I thought, at my huge canvases. And in a moment, the lightning-bolt of inspiration struck.

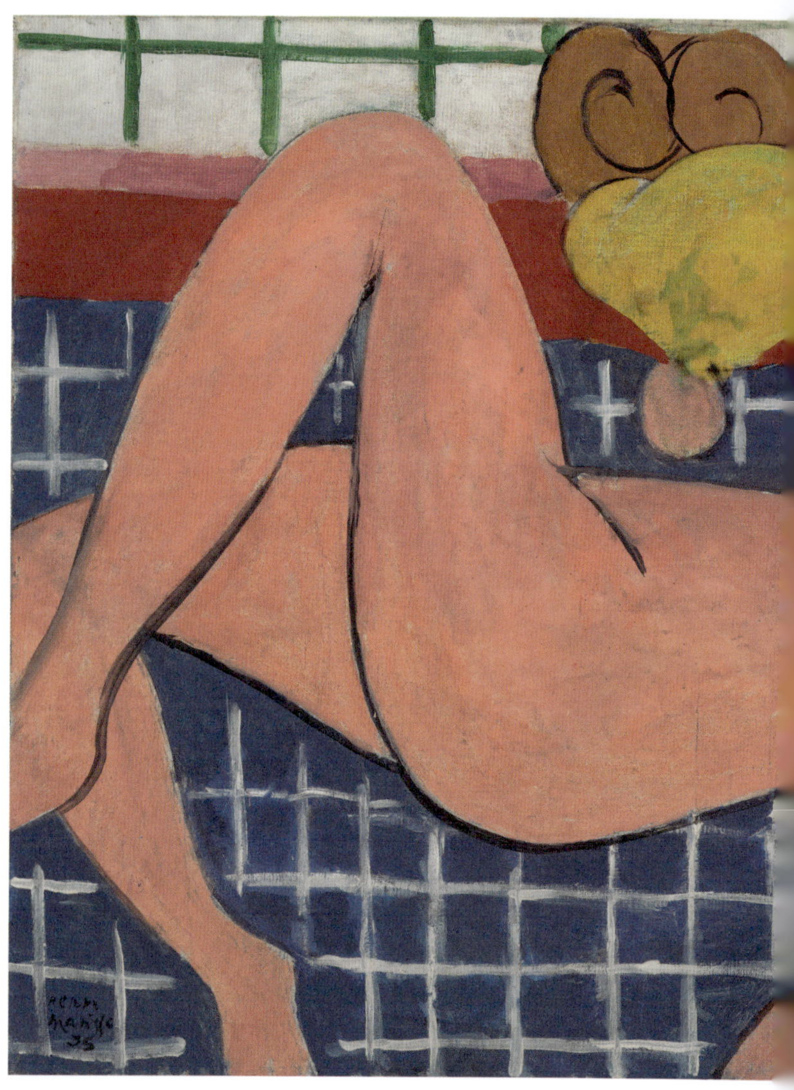

Large Reclining Nude, 1935.
Oil on canvas, 66.4 × 93.3 cm (26⅛ × 36¾ in.).

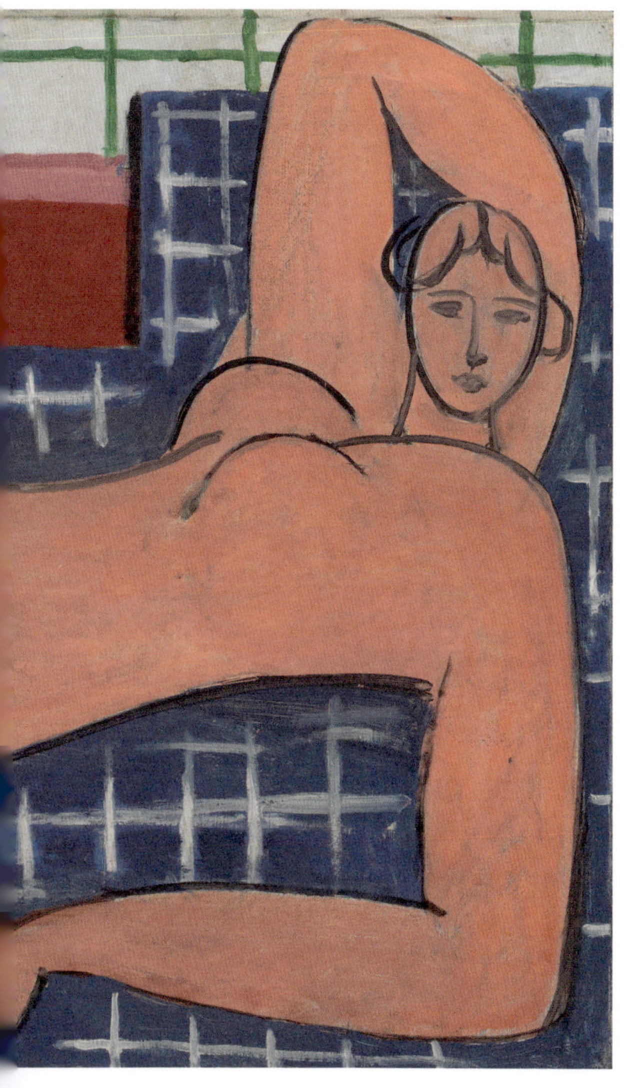

I am not interested in individual items ... but the relationships between ... me, my model, this object, that other object ... small worlds that must find ways to harmonize.

•

I took possession of the surface with the power of my imagination, nothing else ... without using the model.

•

I have not worked for at least two weeks, and so as not to sink into utter darkness ... I took a model and did a nude. This morning, our second sitting, and the difficulties begin.

•

I am satisfied with my drawing.... But my painting is held in check by the new conventions of flat expanses of colour ... which must interact to suggest light, space, and mood.

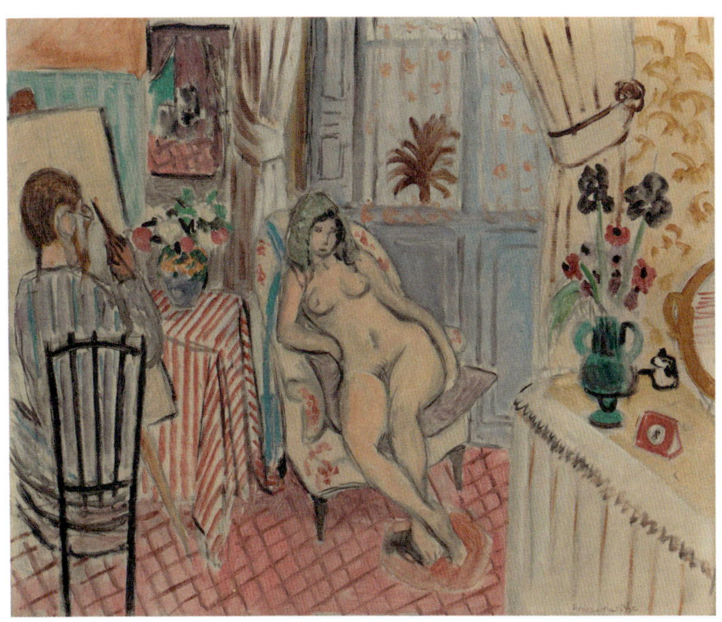

The Artist and Nude Model, 1919. Oil on canvas,
60 × 73 cm (23⅝ × 28¾ in.).

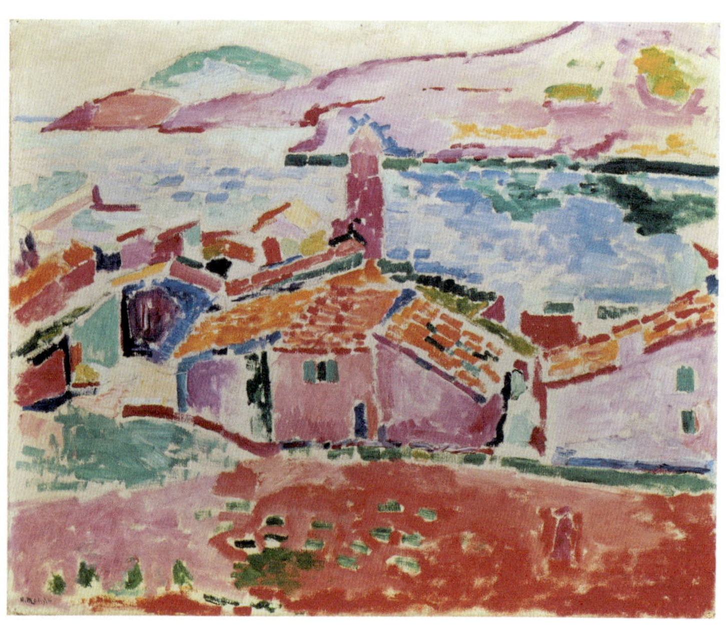

Rooftops of Collioure, 1905. Oil on canvas, 59.5 × 73 cm (23⅜ × 29 in.).

Light is felt and expressed by means of colour, drawing, etc. You create an equivalent, not an imitation. You cannot copy light.

All colours sing together; they have the essential force of a choir. They are like a musical chord.

Colour is a force. My pictures are composed of four or five colours that collide and generate a sense of energy.

A colourist's drawing is not a painting. I must find its equivalent in colour. And that I cannot do at present.

I have been constantly tormented by painting ... perhaps because of the colour of this country, where it is difficult to do shadows in black, unless you deliberately shade your eyes.

I feel I have come
as far as I am able
along the path
to abstraction....
For the moment,
I can go no further.

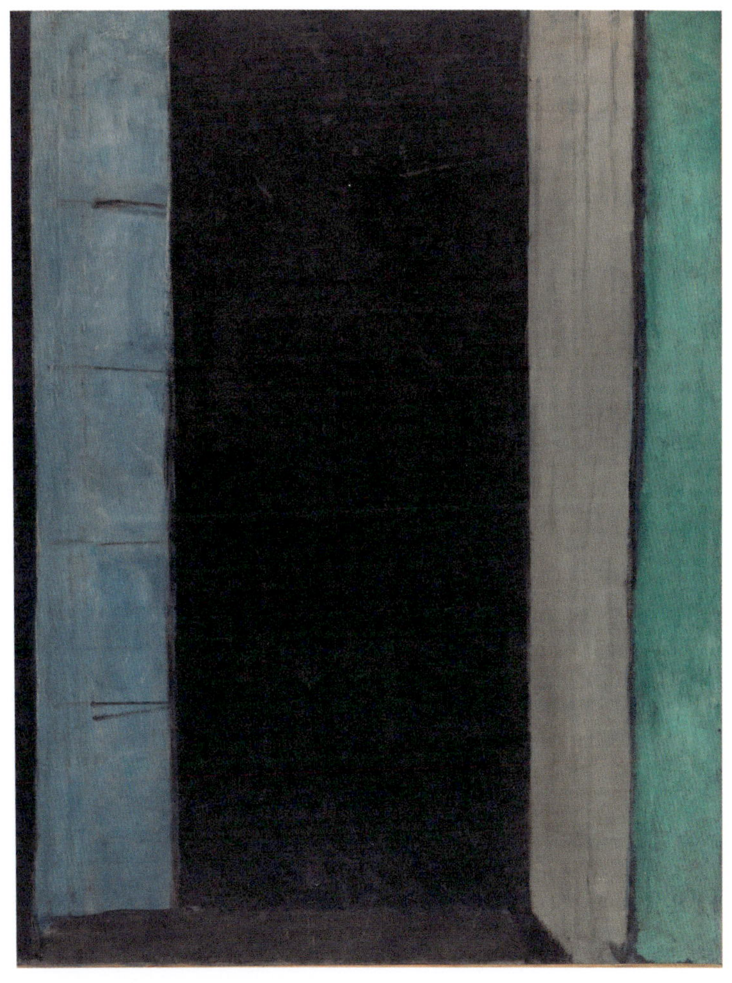

French Window, Collioure, 1914.
Oil on canvas, 116.5 × 89 cm (46 × 35½ in.).

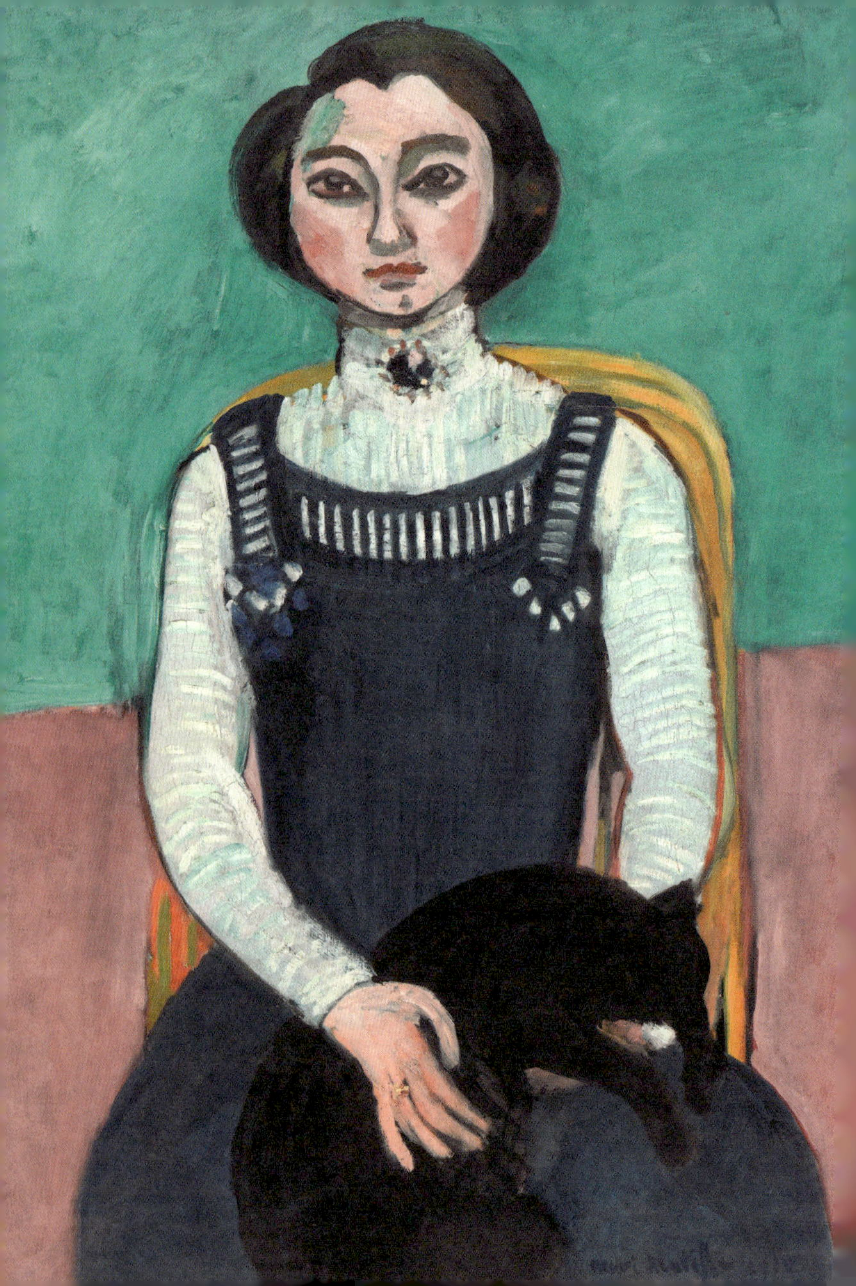

FAMILY AND FRIENDS

In the beginning, when so many were against me ... I was supported by the devoted love of my wife, who was always beside me with all her heart, knew how to listen to my woes, and how to set me back on my feet when I needed it.

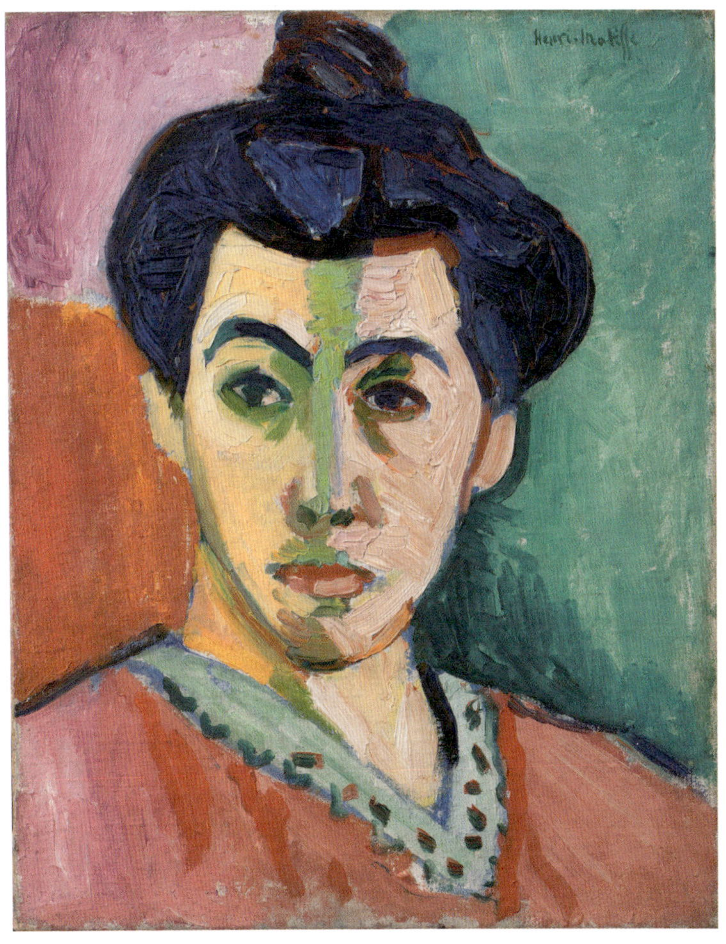

Portrait of Madame Matisse (The Green Stripe), 1916.
Oil and tempera on canvas, 40.5 × 32.5 cm ($15\frac{7}{8}$ × $12\frac{3}{4}$ in.).

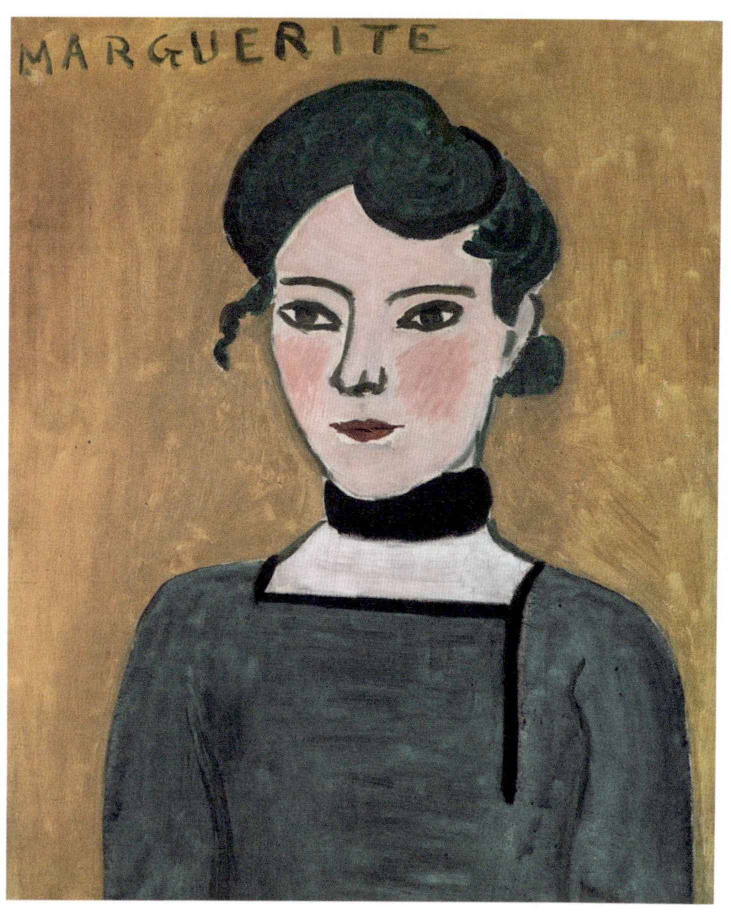

Portrait of Marguerite, 1906–7.
Oil on canvas, 65.1 × 54 cm (25½ × 21¼ in.).

Eight days ago on Saturday [July 1901] we had to perform a tracheotomy on Marguerite. And since then, I have felt sick at heart about everything, especially painting.

Marguerite ... still has the canula and will probably keep it for some time.

Marguerite is very well, it seems the operation is a success, but they make her suffer with each dressing. It is a serious business.

Impossible to come to Naples, the children are sick (mumps) and the house is upside down.... The weather has turned fine and I am working. It is always so hard.

Be more than a chum to your children, be a father to them, always.... It's hard, but it's your duty.

My children
are with me,
Marguerite and
Pierre, which is
a delight, but still,
I work better
when I am alone.

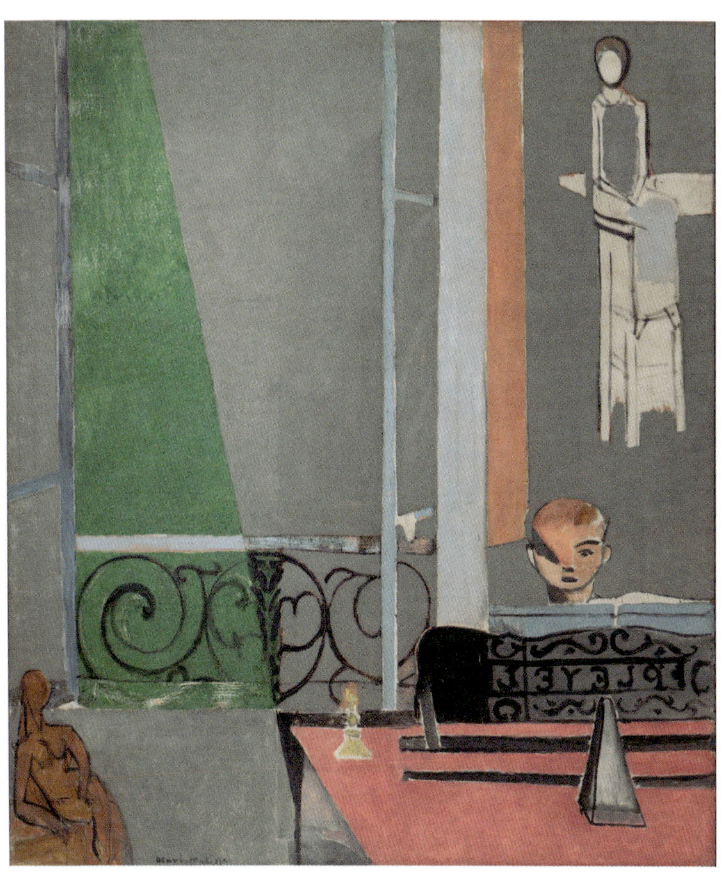

The Piano Lesson, 1916. Oil on canvas, 245.1 × 212.7 cm (96½ × 83¾ in.).

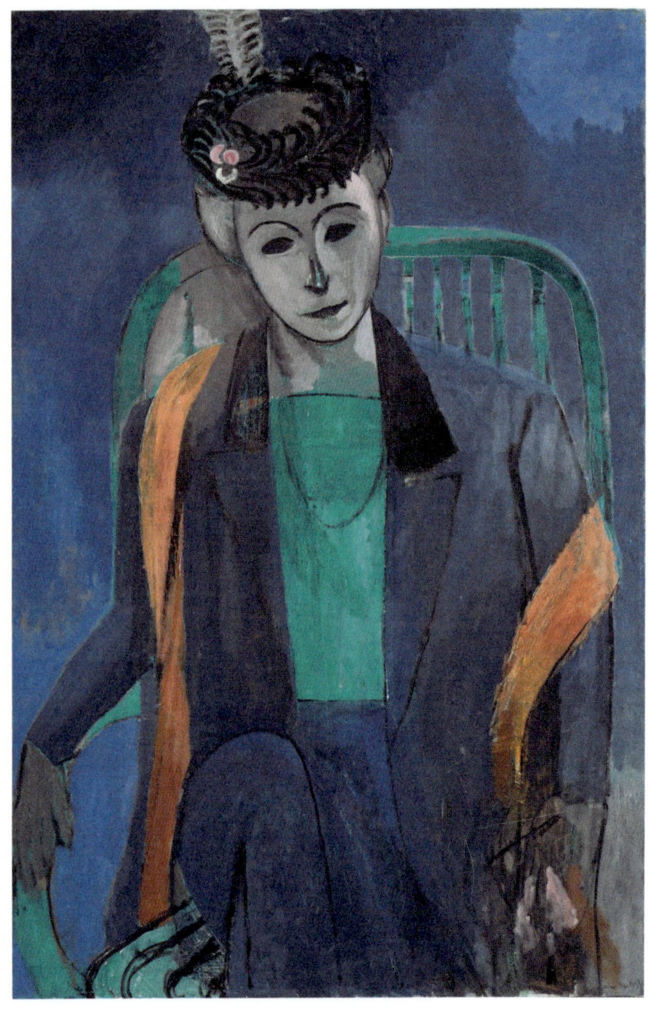

Portrait of the Artist's Wife, 1913. Oil on canvas, 146 × 97.7 cm (57½ × 38½ in.).

By chance ... the portrait of my wife is something of a success with the avant-garde. But I'm still dissatisfied.... It is the beginning of a considerable, painful effort.

To think, I have my whole family more or less settled and all right, a rarity at our age. We have good friends – who can ask for more?

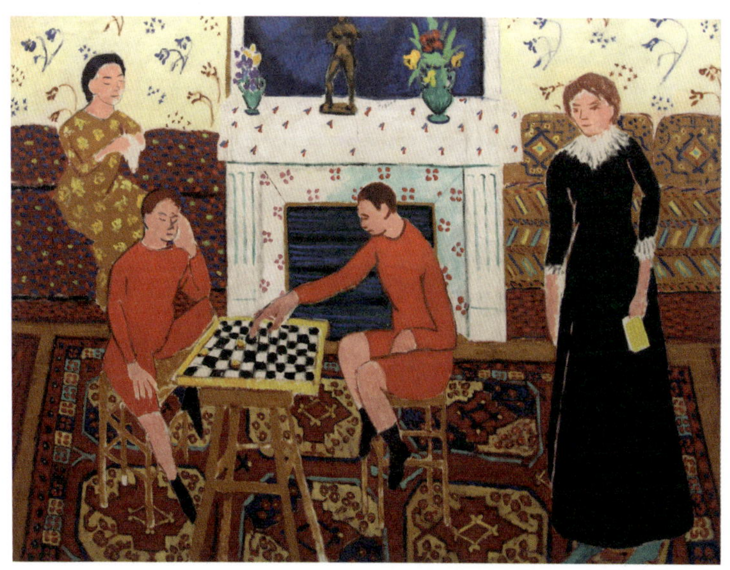

Painter's Family, 1911. Oil on canvas,
143 × 194 cm (56¼ × 76⅜ in.).

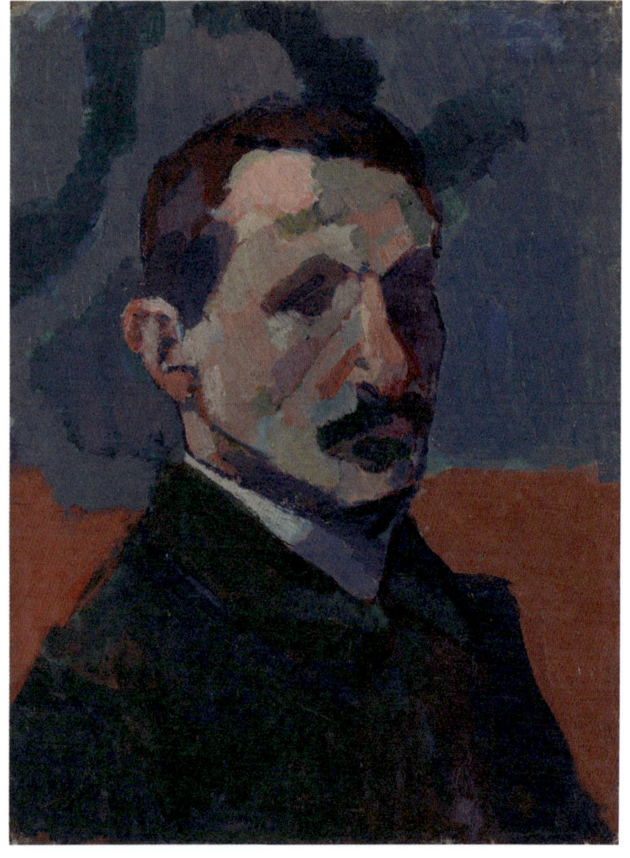

Portrait of Marquet, 1905.
Oil on wood, 31.2 × 41.5 cm (12¼ × 16⅜ in.).

When will you be back? The time is beginning to drag, without my friends. [to Charles Camoin]

My dear friend, I shall seal the envelope on these scribblings without reading them back, because if I did, I would probably never send them. Accept them quite simply as a proof of friendship. [to Charles Camoin]

I don't write to my friends as often as I should, for good reason, as you see here. [to Charles Camoin]

I have a horror of letter-writing, and it's only getting worse. [to Charles Camoin]

I hardly ever take a walk without thinking of the pleasure it would be to share it with you. [to Albert Marquet]

It's all very well to think about those we love, but it's good to see one another again. [to Albert Marquet]

Remember, you sold a picture for one franc, and I had to threaten the buyer on the doorstep of 10 quai Saint-Martin to get him to pay? [to Albert Marquet]

I can see us now, sitting in the Luxembourg gardens.... You were painting the Palace ... which I still have; kids running all around us, criticizing our work. At least they were looking! [to Albert Marquet]

How precious your visit was to me. We relived together moments from our youth that we will probably never ... relive again. [to Georges Rouault]

My dear Rouault ... Pierre tells me your two son-in-laws are both imprisoned. I share your torment.

I am turning to you, old friend, for news of my son Jean, twenty-one years old.... He lives in a suburb that has been badly bombed, and has sent no news of his family, nor his mother and Marguerite.... I'm too worried to do any serious work. [to Charles Camoin]

Madame Matisse remained in Fresnes for three months and was sentenced to three months in prison, on top of her current detention. She has borne them courageously. [to Albert Marquet]

Marguerite was held in secret in Rennes until the month of August, then sent to Belfort, from where she took to the mountains.... The doctor said it is a miracle she got through it all so well. [to Albert Marquet]

Fortunately, I am with Madame Lydia, and we shall probably return by plane. It would not surprise me at all to discover that she knows how to fly.
[to André Rouveyre]

When I am bored, I do a portrait of Madame Lydia; I know her to the letter.

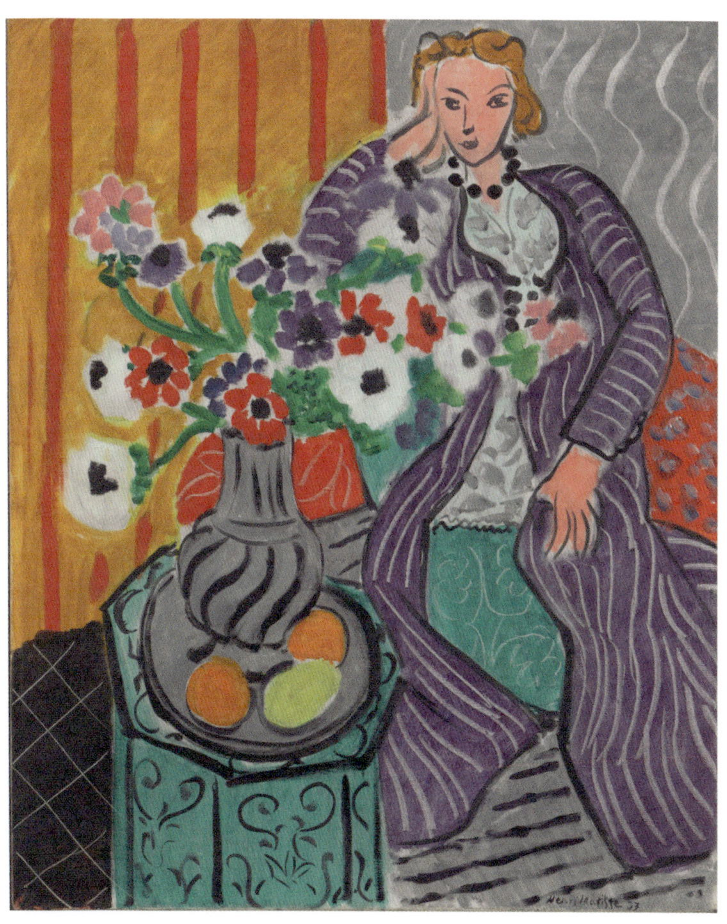

Purple Robe and Anemones, 1937.
Oil on canvas, 73 × 60 cm (28¾ × 23 in.).

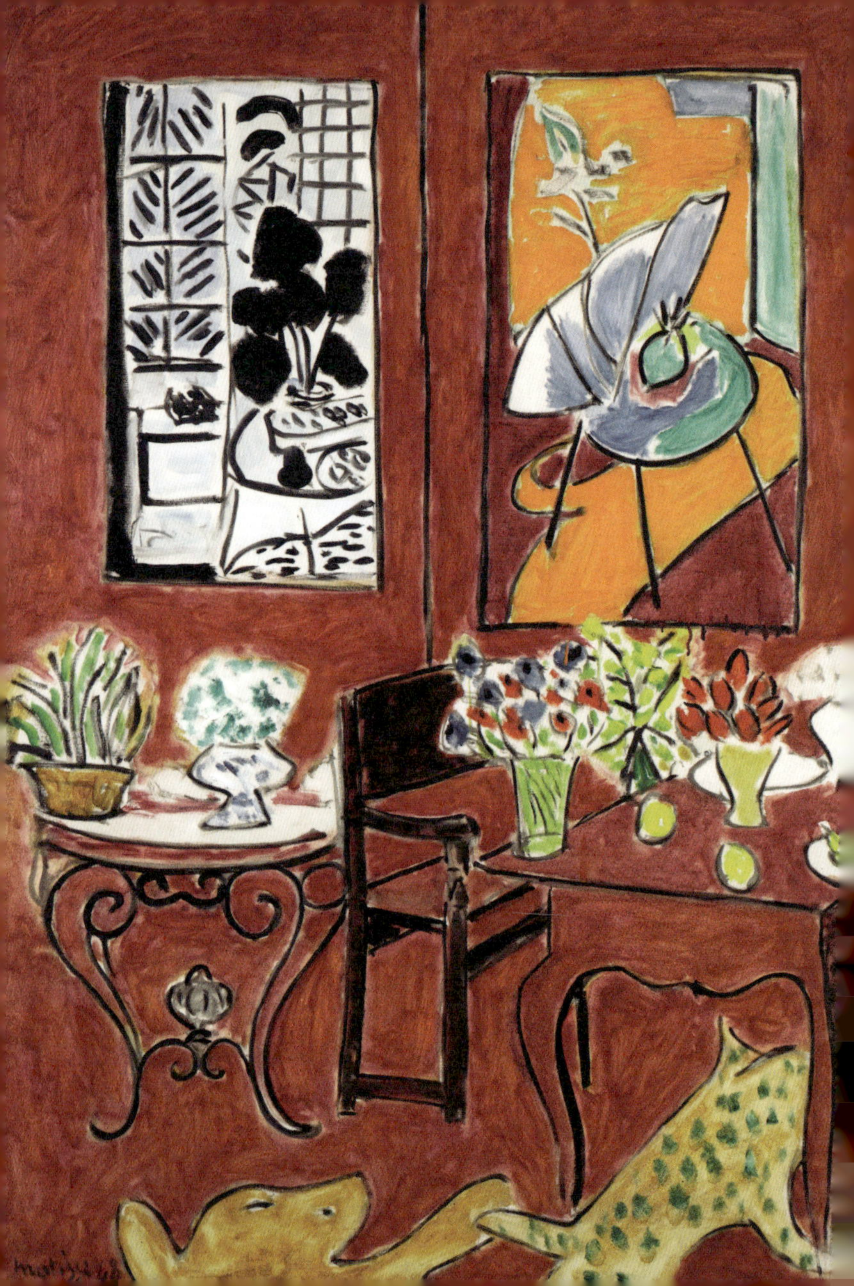

HOME COMFORTS

The pleasant company of the objects that surround me ... Towards them, I feel affection without pain (which is the risk in other areas of life).

The charm of an open window ... My sense that the space from the horizon to my interior is one and the same. The boat sailing by lives in the same space as the familiar objects around me ... not two different worlds.

I spend a lot of time on small things in the garden, here in Vence. I'm on very good terms with a pomegranate tree that's in blossom ... [and] an old field of artichokes whose leaves form arabesques ... and irises ... and a fig tree whose leaves, so delicious to the eye, make me draw.

We know, in our mind, the scent of violets or hyacinths ... but it's good to experience it in real life. And wine, and tobacco and all the rest.

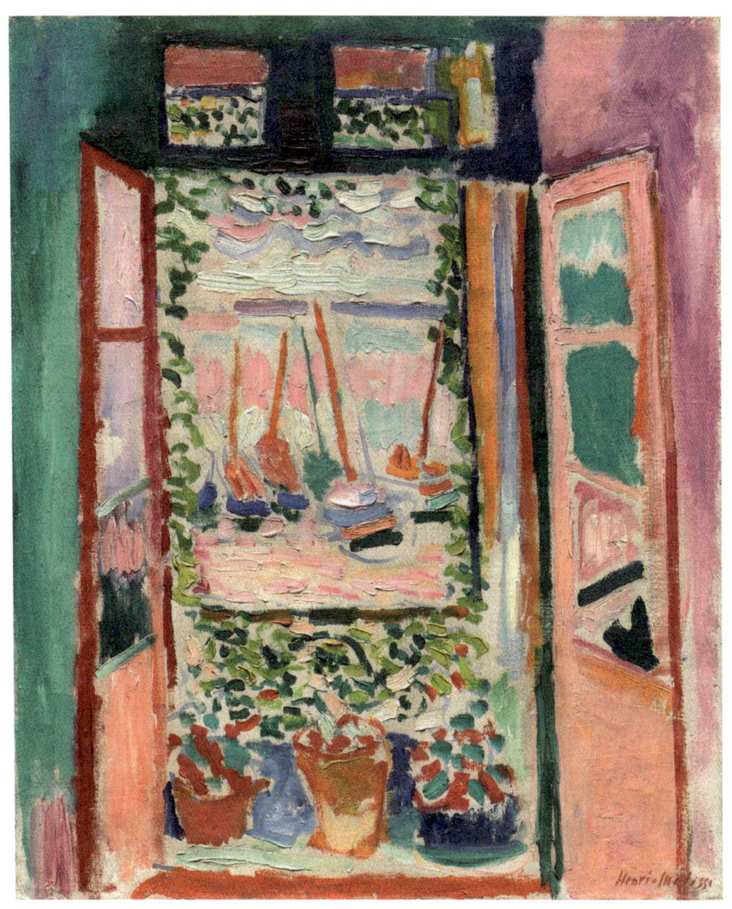

Open Window, Collioure, 1905. Oil on canvas, 55.3 × 46 cm (21¾ × 18⅛ in.).

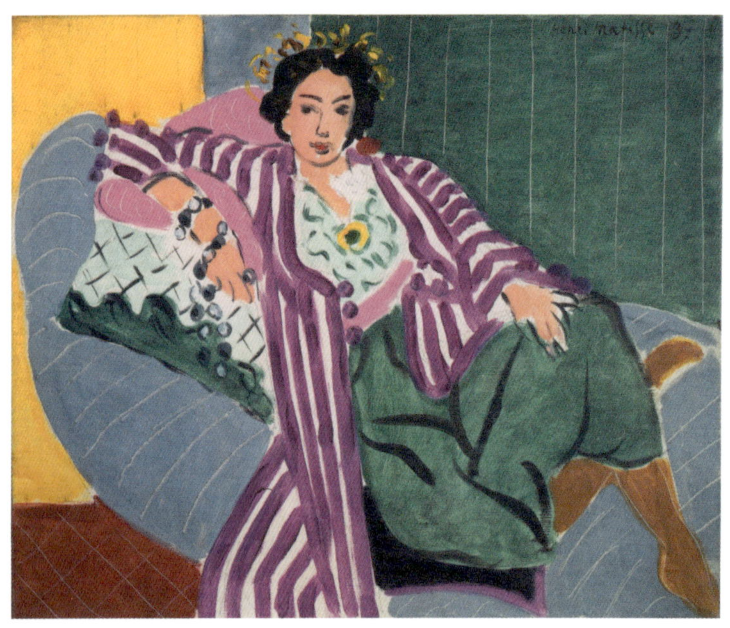

Small Odalisque in a Purple Robe, 1937.
Oil on canvas, 38.1 × 45.7 cm (15 × 18 in.).

Hurrah for joy, and fried potato chips!

…

... delicious painterly flavours ...

…

The oranges you sent arrived yesterday ... despite the long journey, only a third are spoiled.... What salads we shall have! Thank you, thank you, thank you!

…

In the very hot weather in Saint-Tropez, we made couch grass-and-liquorice lemonade. I recommend it. Signac knows the recipe.

…

I've arranged ... for three or four young, pretty models ... to pose individually for drawings, three hours in the morning, three hours in the afternoon. That's what keeps me here, amid the flowers and fruit, with which I am gently, imperceptibly making contact.

I've decided not to leave Nice – my life is here within my studio walls.

I planned to paint flowers and fruit.... I have several arrangements around my studio – but in these uncertain times ... I dread ... the tête-à-tête with objects that I alone must bring to life.

Once I've bought an object, there's something missing: my yearning for it.

If I think something isn't going well, I seek out a satisfying corner and find that I've little to complain about.

Sometimes a motif gives me pause, a corner of the studio that speaks to me, even if it's beyond me at the time, and I wait for the thunderclap of inspiration that's sure to come.

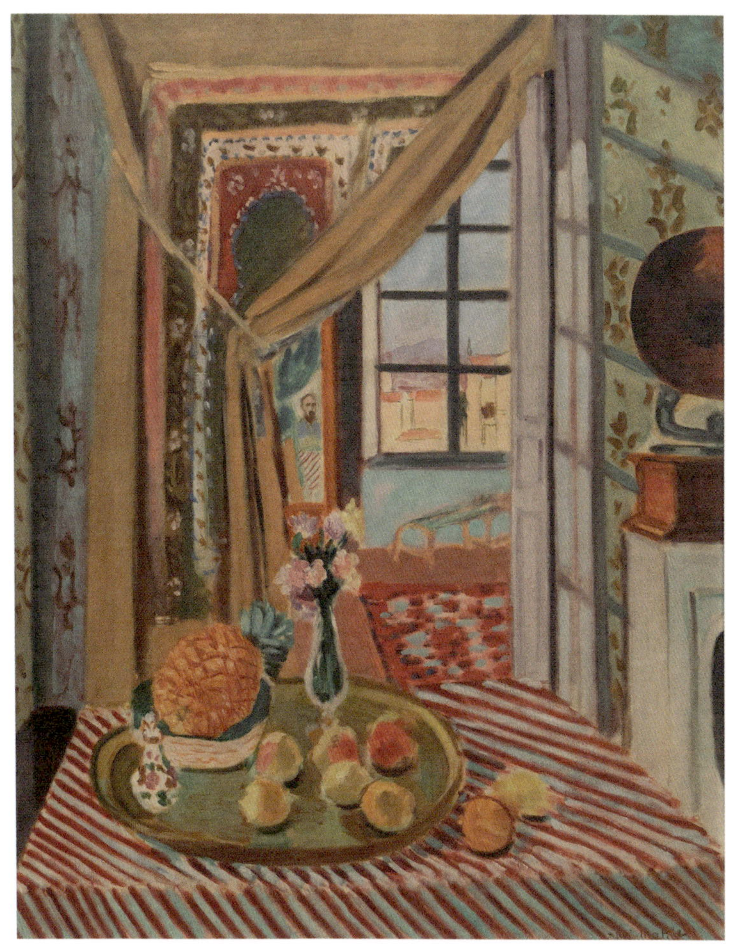

Interior with Phonograph, 1924. Oil on canvas, 100.5 × 80 cm (39½ × 31½ in.).

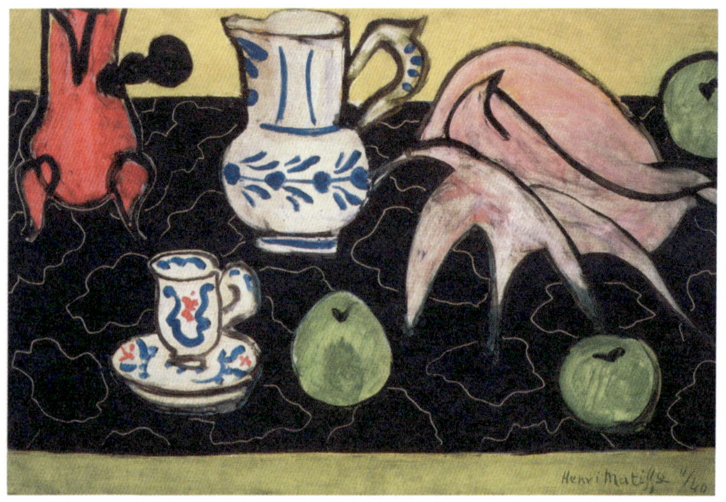

Still Life with Seashell on Black Marble, 1940.
Oil on canvas, 54 × 81 cm (21¼ × 31⅞ in.).

A still life with a seashell, a pot with blue flowers, a coffee cup, a coffee pot, and three green apples on a black and green marble table ... worked (transformed) over thirty sittings.

Lately, we have rediscovered the emotional, decorative properties of lines and colours thanks to the work of modern artists. Our department stores are overrun with fabrics showing outsized scribbled, abstract motifs.

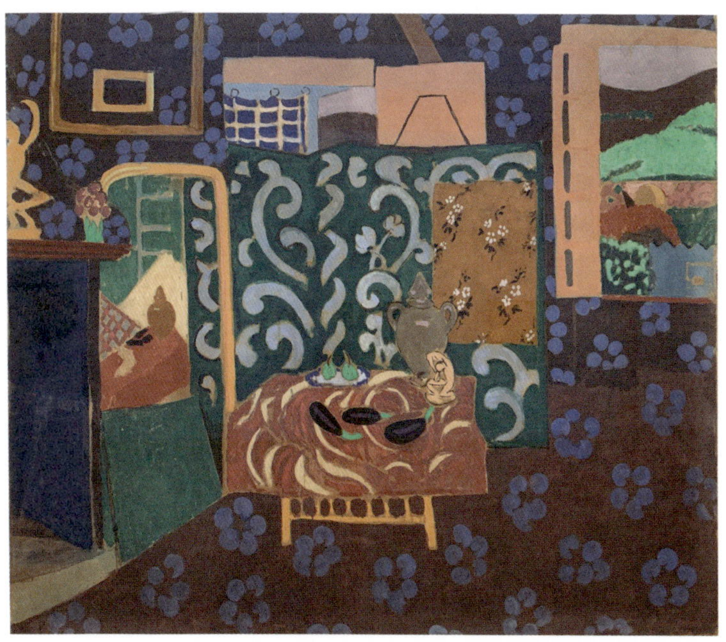

Interior with Aubergines, 1911.
Oil on canvas, 212 × 246 cm (83½ × 96⅞ in.).

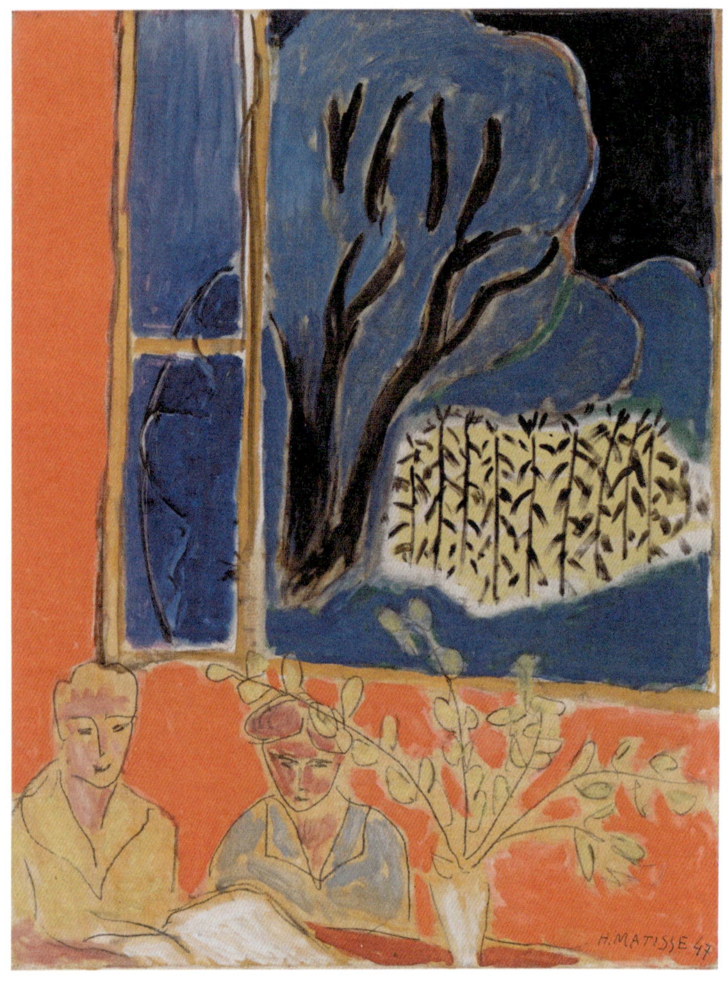

Two Young Girls in a Coral Interior, Blue Garden, 1947.
Oil on canvas, 64.8 × 49.8 cm (25½ × 19⅝ in.).

I dream of an art that is balanced, pure, tranquil, devoid of unsettling or troubling subject-matter ... that soothes, and calms the mind, the way a good armchair relaxes our tired bodies.

I'm in bed, two models are close by, in front of the garden window, and I live in the light that unites both settings.

Eight days seeing no one at all. A thoroughly good thing.

Work, books, and a radio ... all a modern hermit needs.

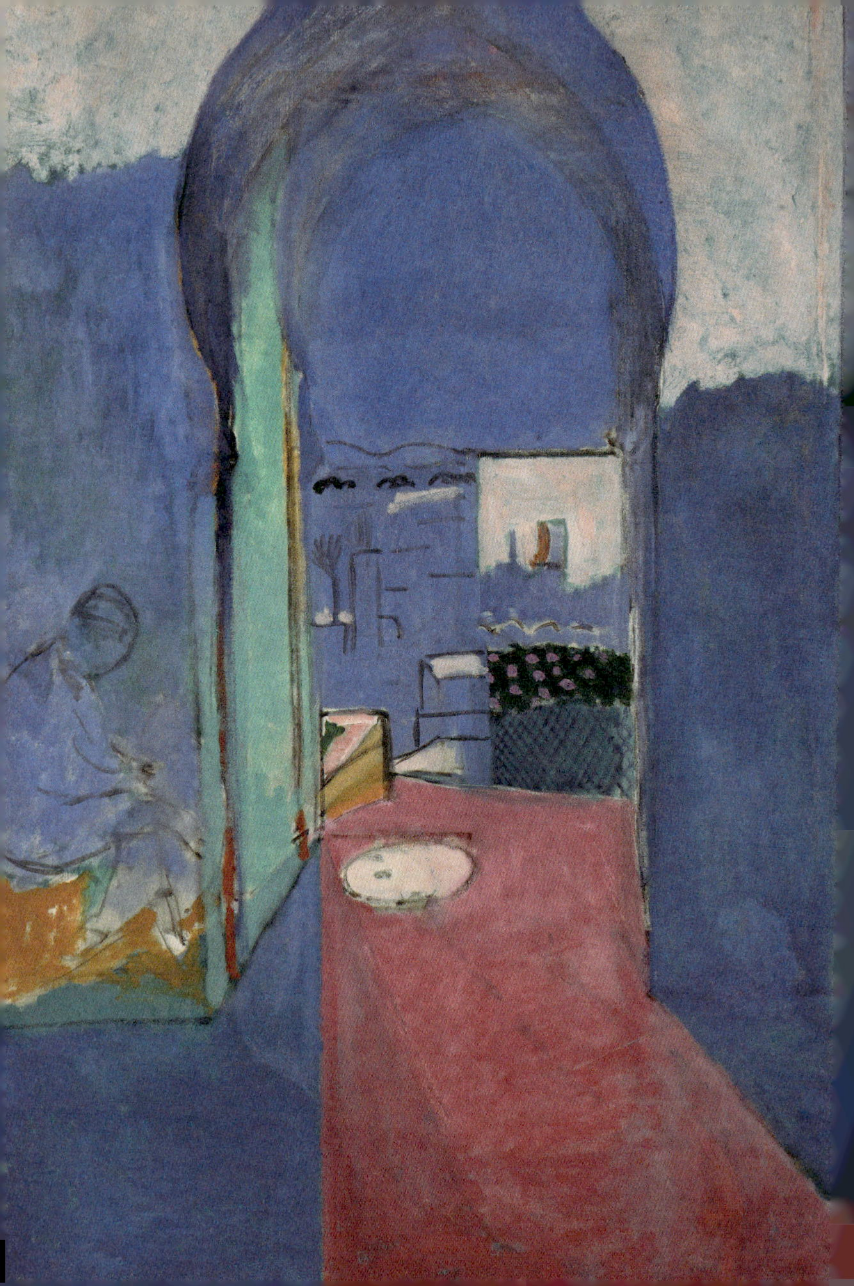

TRAVEL

In Belle-Île-en-Mer … I appreciated the luminous Impressionist palette, mixing all the colours of the prism.

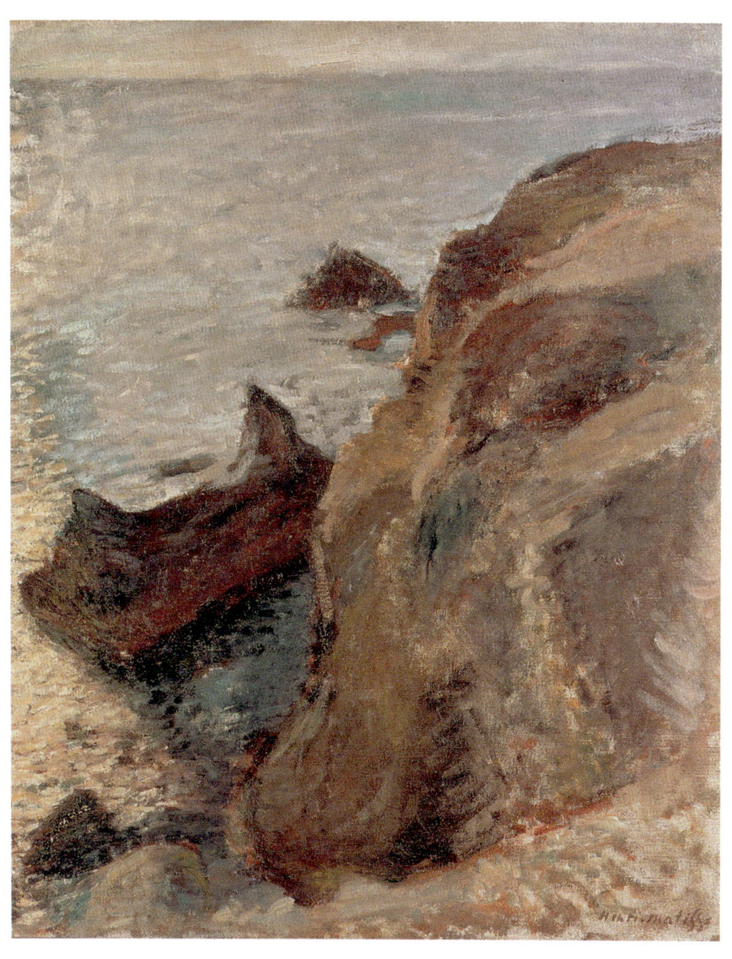

Rocks and the Sea, 1897.
Oil on canvas, 65 × 53.9 cm (25¾ × 21¼ in.).

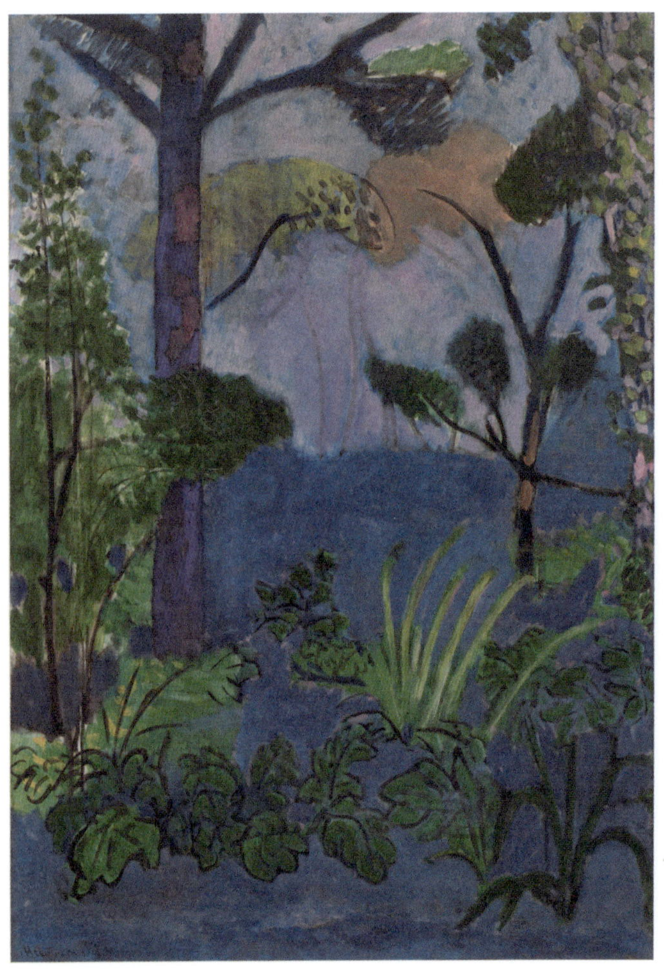

Moroccan Landscape, 1912. Oil on canvas,
115 × 80 cm (45¼ × 31½ in.).

Almost every one of my paintings is an adventure.

The travels in Morocco helped me ... reconnect with nature better than was possible while applying a lively but rather limited theory such as Fauvism.

The most amazing, bulbous flowers sprang up ... and the hills around Tangiers, which were the colour of lion skins, turned the most extraordinary green, with stormy skies like a painting by Delacroix.

We ... went down into a beautiful, very broad valley, filled with grasses ... up to the mules' necks, and tall daisies, and buttercups, and we walked through this sea of flowers, as if no one had ever passed that way before.

The Moroccan winter – apart from the lack of cold – is just the same as in Paris. Why did I put myself through it?

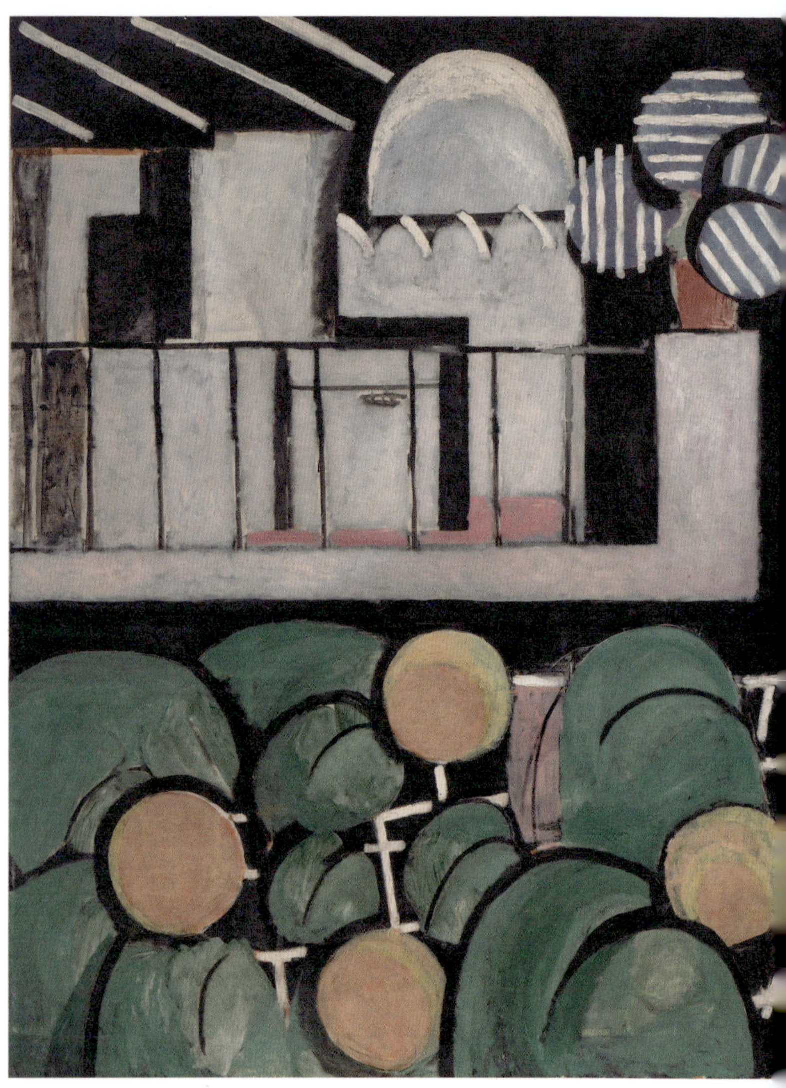

The Moroccans, 1924. Oil on canvas, 181.3 × 279.4 cm (71⅜ × 110 in.).

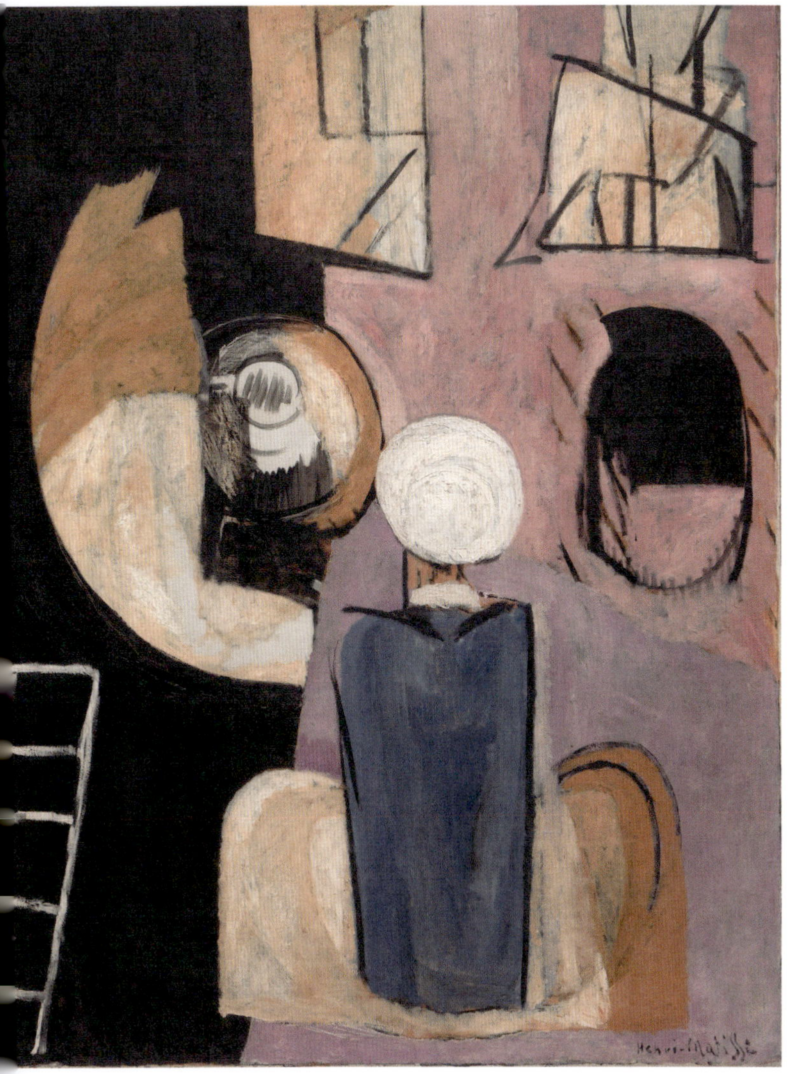
Henri-Matisse

The desert ... so inhuman. Lions and tigers no longer roam, but had they appeared, I should hardly have been less terrified.

No women anywhere. Bundled in white sheets, like First Communion Day in Nice.

I shall not be staying here much longer. The rain will soon be back.

After watching the rain fall for fifteen days ... we're basking in the fine weather and utterly luxuriant vegetation.

Bad weather is on the way, and I wonder if I wouldn't be better off somewhere less wet and windy, like Collioure, Barcelona, or Corsica.

Corsica ... Almond trees in blossom amid silvery olive trees and the sea, blue, blue, so very blue.

Dark-green orange trees set with fruit like gemstones, the tall eucalyptus with variegated foliage like a cockerel's plumage ... And almost always in the background, high mountains with snowy peaks.

The sad sky has got the better of me, and I'm leaving for a short trip to the Midi, where most likely I'll stay.

The temperature! I've never felt so hot in Collioure.

I reached Nice ten days ago after a very difficult journey. I got straight to work, to get back on an even keel.

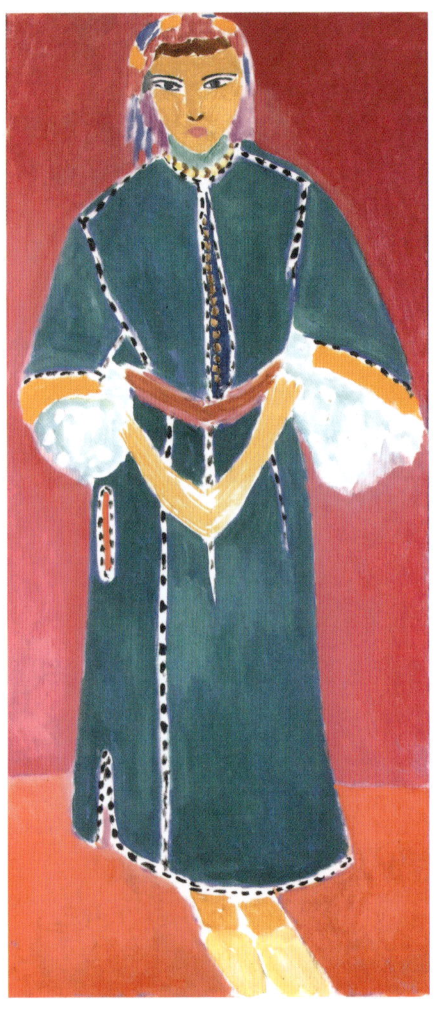

Zorah Standing, 1912. Oil on canvas, 146.5 × 61 cm (57⅝ × 24 in.).

Have you been to Spain? Take some time to breathe.

Shchukin told me, 'You know the Mediterranean, and Africa, a little, but you don't know Asia, and you'll get an idea of Asia in Moscow.'

Moscow is Asian. A big village with wooden houses, a palace or two, and two or three churches on every street ... the cobbles all uneven, and when it rains, puddles like great lakes make it difficult to get about.

A simple journey from Paris to London by plane is a revelation.... We'll remember ... the splendour of the sun, and the unlimited space in which we felt so free.

Shouldn't all young people take a long plane journey at the end of their studies?

RITZ TOWER, PARK AVENUE AND 57TH STREET, NEW YORK, 37TH FLOOR

New York is marvellous. I am thirty years younger. Why travel any further?

New York City is vast and majestic, like the sea – with a powerful sense of human effort and enterprise.

In Tahiti, there's no trouble, no bother, nothing, just ennui, so that the Europeans long for 5 p.m. when they can get drunk.

Twenty days on a coral island: pure light, pure air, pure colour. Sapphire blue, turquoise, emerald.

The memories of Tahiti are only coming back to me now, fifteen years later, as hypnotic, obsessive images: sea urchins, corals, fish, birds, jellyfish, sponges ...

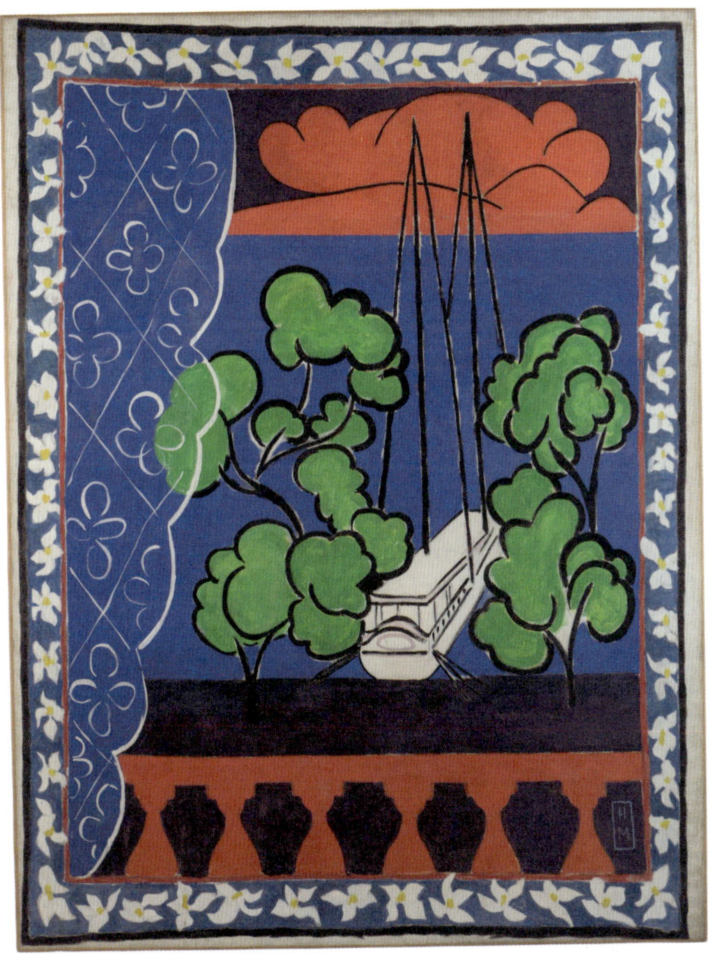

Window at Tahiti or Tahiti II, 1935–6.
Gouache and tempera on canvas, 238 × 183 cm (93¾ × 72 in.).

Have done absolutely nothing except take bad photos.... Shall be happy to see France again.

I stopped in Martinique on my way back from Tahiti ... and remembered why I had longed for Tahiti for twenty years. The light!

It takes a day to cross through the Panama Canal, like going from northern to southern France: you see the difference in the light.

When you emerge from the isthmus of Panama into the Caribbean, the intoxicating quality of light in the Pacific is no more.

I've been everywhere from Moscow to Tangiers ... but France is like a garden, an extraordinary bouquet of flowers, in the midst of all that.

No more Dakar ...
No more desert
No more camels
The amazing forest of Fontainebleau! Vast!
Oh, the moonlit nights among the tall trees,
in the clearings, ah!

The excitement of Paris will be enough for now.

I've been to the Parc de la Tête d'Or in Lyon.... The tropical greenhouses have a dreamlike quality when a shaft of sunlight pierces the wildly decorative foliage.

Lyon is a city of substance, but Nice is a stage set,
a fragile thing, very beautiful.

Nice is the city of a few dreamers, but mostly
jewellers, hôteliers, and beautiful young women.

People only come to Nice to relax, gamble, stroll on the promenade, and they soon tire of that.... 'What shall we do? We did Monte Carlo yesterday, Cannes the day before. Where can we go now?'

Nice's rich, silvery, bright light, especially in the lovely month of January, seems ... invaluable to the spirit of a visual artist, especially a painter.

To make my pictures, I need several days straight with the same sensations ... and I find that uncomplicated climate nowhere but the Côte d'Azur.

I feel that what's needed for now is a spell of concentrated work: travel, a different climate, and the excitement of new things ... picturesque landscapes ... would bring only distraction.

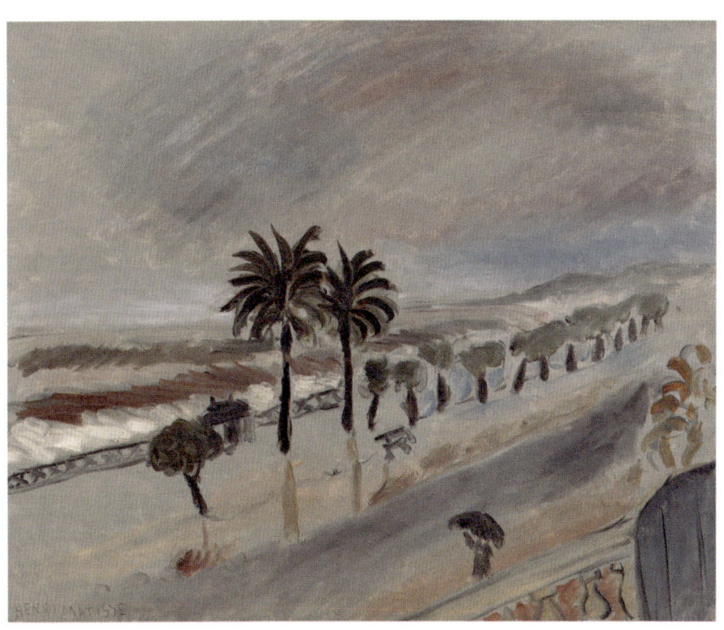

Storm at Nice, 1919–20. Oil on canvas, 60.5 × 73.5 cm (23⅞ × 28⅞ in.).

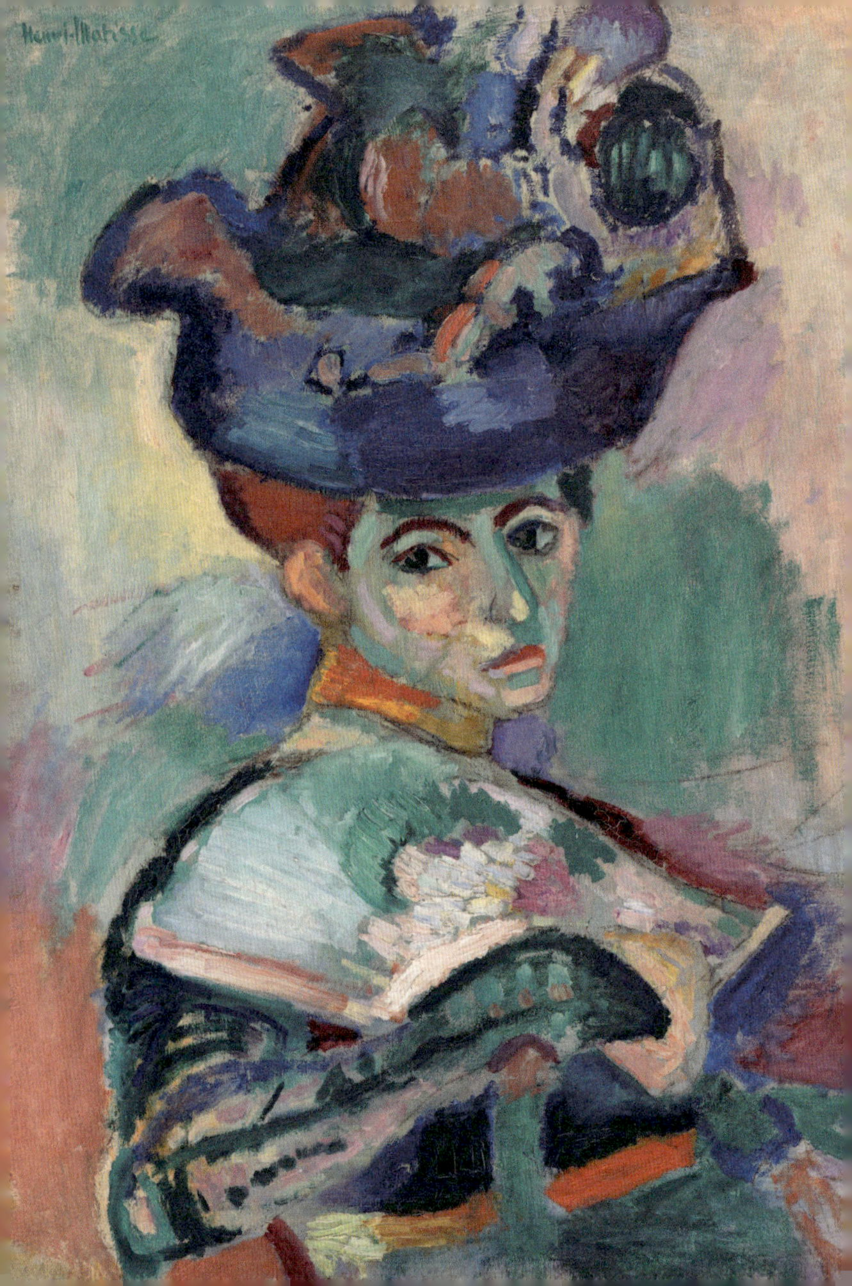
Henri-Matisse

FAME AND REBELLION

If there is no public, there is no artist .... You would not paint on a desert island.

The audience is the medium you work with.... The fellow ... who tells you 'Monsieur Matisse, I can't tell you how much I love your picture' ... an ordinary working man who's never spent a cent on a painting.

Your audience are not art buyers. They are the responsive, receptive medium upon which you hope to make your mark.

You need to know how to keep something back from people. Do not accustom them to overfamiliarity.

Once people have met you, they say, 'Oh yes, so-and-so, he's charming!' And from that moment on, you no longer hold the same fascination, the same attraction.

When you work to please other people, you achieve nothing.

You had the honour of being invited to the Salon d'Automne, while I got nothing! [to Albert Marquet]

Our old friends ... are scared I will ridicule their terribly serious exhibition of paintings by sending along a wanton nymph – my speciality.

At 55 ... I discovered canoeing.... 134 outings in one year.... I was presented with a real gold medal. The only medal I have ever received!

When so many people were against me ... I avoided sterile, all-consuming hatred, and that kept my spirit bright and clean.

I felt grazed and sore ... but what kept me going was the idea ... that I had failed to express clearly what I wanted to say.

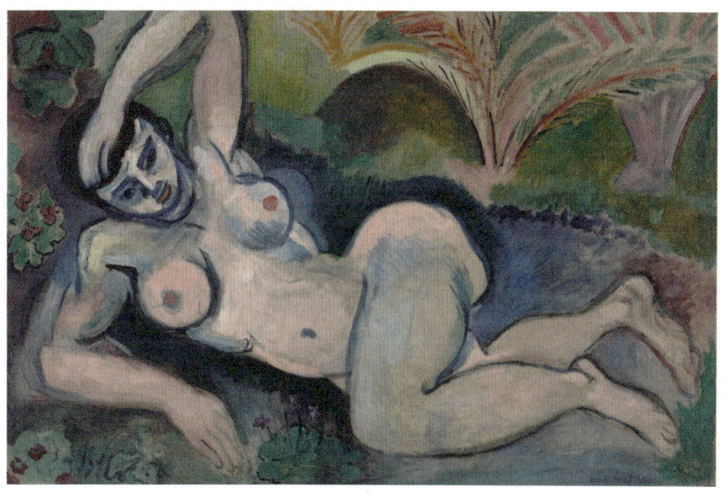

The Blue Nude (Souvenir of Biskra), 1907.
Oil on canvas, 92.1 × 140.3 cm (36¼ × 55¼ in.).

Once I had shown clearly what I wanted to do, people would be touched, and my reputation unchallenged.

The most demanding, competitive examination will leave an artist, even once he has passed, at around thirty years of age, with an inauthentic mind, limited sensibility and skill.

The Prix de Rome should be abolished. It is fundamentally sterile, even harmful.... It steers young artists away from their natural, instinctive path.

I have seen painters return from the French School in Rome, horrified by the sudden realization that they are utterly incapable of authentic self-expression.

An artist has no greater enemies than his own worst paintings.

I believe an artist's character develops, asserts itself in the struggles that it endures with other personalities.... If the artist dies in the fight, it is because he was not meant to survive.

Think of all the people who have 'made it',
who when they remember their early difficulties
declare 'those were the good times'.

You have to be able to repeat a masterpiece, start over again, prove you were not merely the plaything of chance or your own nervous state.

Didn't Japanese artists of the golden era change their name several times in their lives? I like that: they wanted to safeguard their freedom.

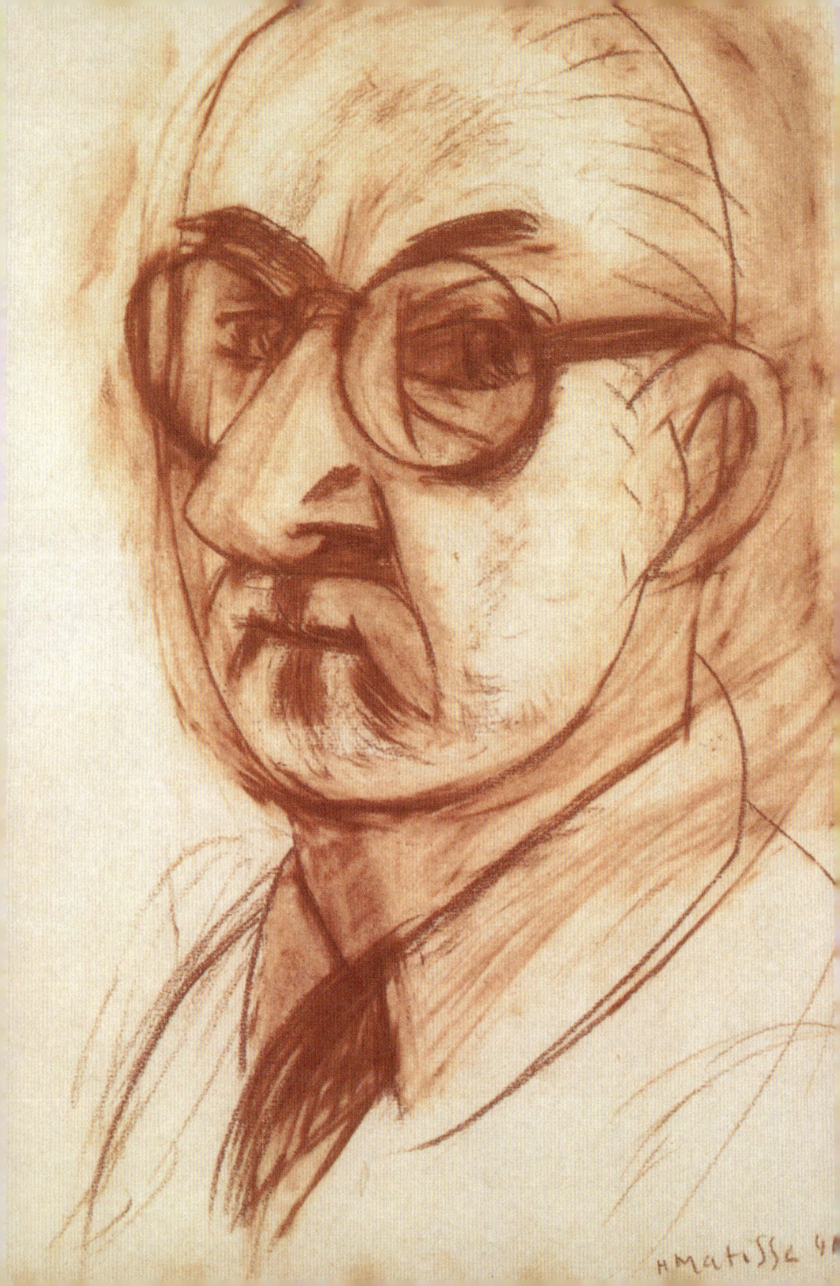
HMatisse

SICKNESS AND OLD AGE

My health has been good for quite long enough, and now I am afraid.

I was so fortunate to be fit enough to work for fifty years, until the age of seventy. What happened then was payment of a kind. Everyone must take their turn. I've paid my dues!... This extreme physical suffering, which I'd never felt before ... made me see how fortunate I had been in life.

The clinic in Lyon was ... a new world ... very humble, straightforward people ... dedicated to snatching those in their care from the jaws of death. At a time when human life is worth so very little.

Thanks to my surgeon's dedication and skill, I came through. It's like being reborn, and now I see time in a completely different way.

I have come back from so distant a shore, the sisters at the clinic called me 'the Resurrected One'.

My doctors are satisfied with my convalescence, but I find it's too slow.... I think my grey cells are working again, and I have a few years' work in me still – the reason why I so longed to be free of this cursed business.

Before the operation ... it galled me not to be able to do several things all at once. I was impatient to finish whatever I was doing and attack something else. I always felt short of time. Since my rebirth, I'm much calmer, more balanced; I take time for self-care.

I have been living in bed for months, and I am not at all bored. I am very happy, even, especially when I have had a full, productive day.

Perhaps after all, without realizing it until now, I believe in a second life... in some paradise where I will create vast frescoes.

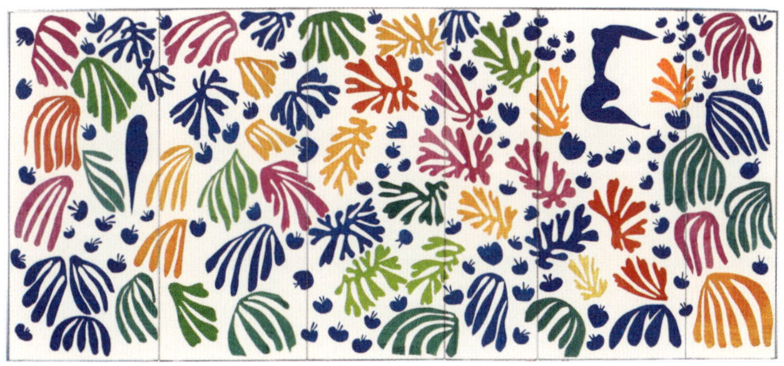

The Parakeet and the Mermaid, 1952–3.
Oil on canvas, 337 × 768.5 cm (132⅝ × 302½ in.).

I never forget a painting, though in working every day for fifty years, I have done quite a few.

When someone mentions one of my paintings, even a very old one ... I see my feelings at that moment with great clarity, and all the colours, and the weight it holds within my work as a whole.

It is no ordinary thing for a man to be able to work until seventy, interested in himself, in the continued development of his mind and character.

I still work a little, and I see there has been no decline in quality, thanks to good discipline. But modesty prevails.

May we not keep our youthful, ardent imagination, till the day we die?

It takes exceptional circumstances for a man to live to seventy with the good fortune to carry on doing what he has always loved with a passion.... We are the lucky ones; never forget it.

To see that Renoir, full of aches and pains ... unable to put one foot in front of the other ... could still find happiness in working, and in talking about his work.

Don't waste the few days that are left to us by weeping for the past.

At our age, we must be careful to avoid bother and irritation, while we still can.

The delight of old age is its heightened sensitivity to fragrance.

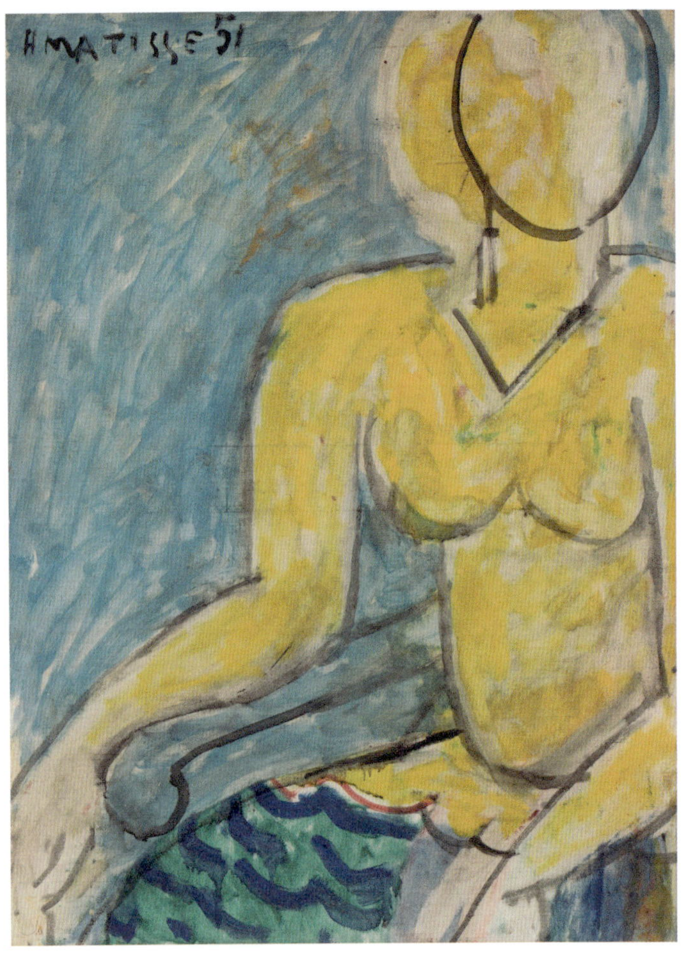

Katia in Yellow Blouse, 1951.
Oil and pencil on canvas, 82.5 × 61 cm (32½ × 24 in.).

We are in everything we do, in our first canvases and our last, just the same.

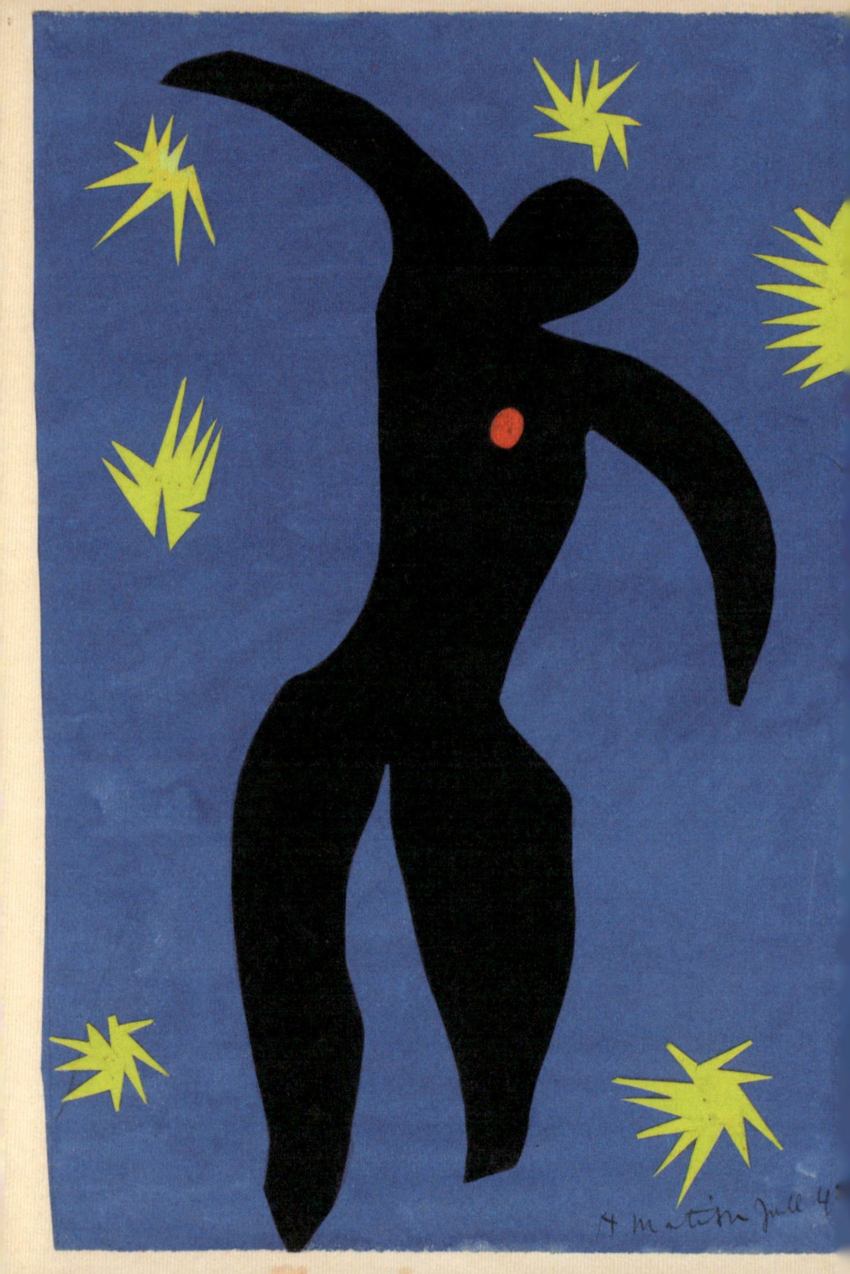

LIFE'S LESSONS

To each his truth,
thank goodness.

Young painters, misunderstood painters, or painters who are only understood late in life: feel no hatred.

Hate is an all-consuming parasite.

No point in rubbing a fellow up the wrong way; take him for what he is.

There is merit in laughing when you really do not want to.

Don't sing out your sorrows, overcome them.

There is always life. Get your teeth into it. Eat, and your appetite will come.

My idea of luxury? Something that can be communicated, shared.

[Luxury] goes far beyond money. It is something within everyone's reach.

Luxury comes with a particular quality of love. It is dressing or undressing your beloved, unforced feeling, devoid of pretence, something that changes you for ever.

I am a romantic, but a good half ... rationalist too – hence the fight from which I emerge triumphant, at times, but gasping for breath.

Style results from the nature and elevation of an artist's spirit, whether ... acquired or developed, or wholly intuitive.

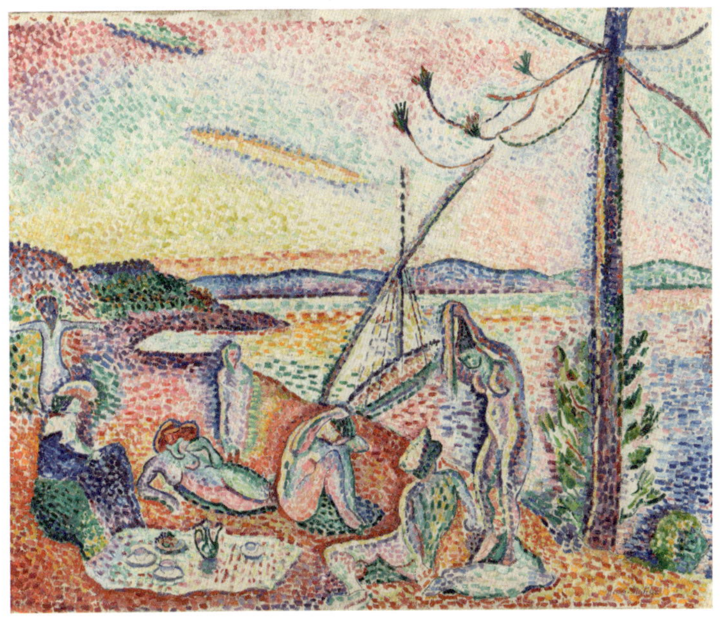

Luxe, Calme et Volupté, 1904.
Oil on canvas, 98.5 × 118.5 cm (37 × 46 in.).

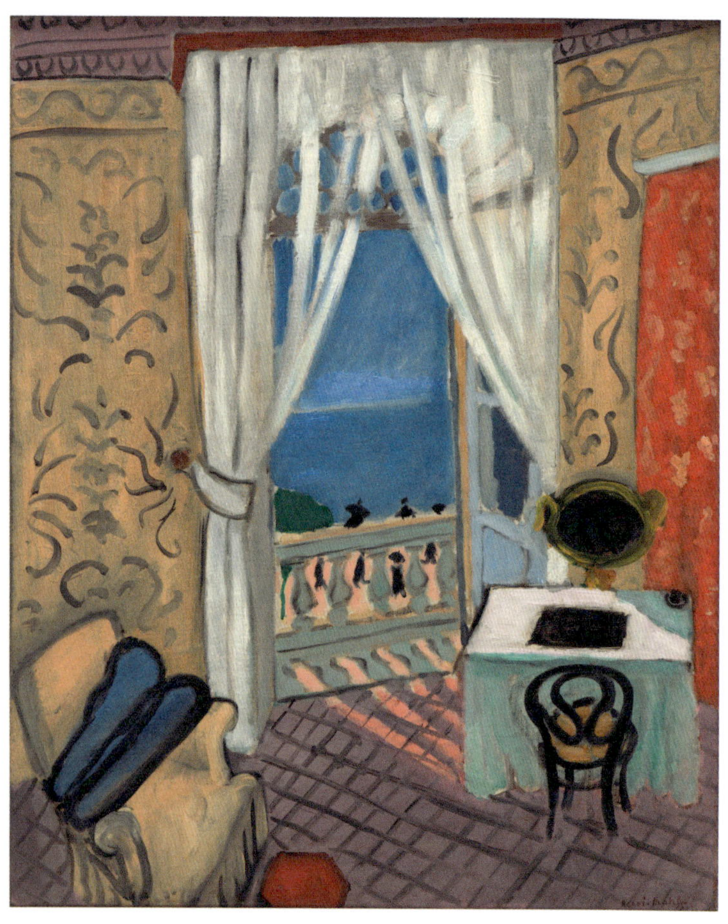

Interior with Violin Case, 1919.
Oil on canvas, 73 × 60 cm (28¾ × 23⅝ in.).

The point of artists is their skill, as they enhance colour and drawing with the richness of their imagination, sublimated by the emotion they feel when they contemplate the beauty of nature, just like a poet or a musician.

I cannot do politics, which alas almost everyone else does, and to make up for it I must do firm, sensitive canvases.

I'm a Bolshevist! Burn the capitalists!! (Tear this letter up!)

In my heart of hearts, I feel we should not inflict suffering on people whose ideas differ from our own. But today that is what they call Freedom.

It is a hard, necessary struggle, all day, every day, to accept the irresponsibility that will set your mind at ease.

Men are always wrong. Just ask women, who are creatures of great good sense.

Bad times make the good times stand out.

If I could, I would throw painting to the devil. It brings very little satisfaction, and far too little money.

Despite what one might think, I have been lucky all my life.... I have always kept busy, always tended to my troubles, and I had no shortage of those. Perhaps, without them, I would have been bored.

I am not a believer, but when things are not going well, I say the prayers I said when I was a child.... It takes me back to a better world.

I have a strong sense of being helped.... But it is like watching a conjuror whose tricks baffle me. And I feel robbed.... I am ungrateful, but unrepentant.

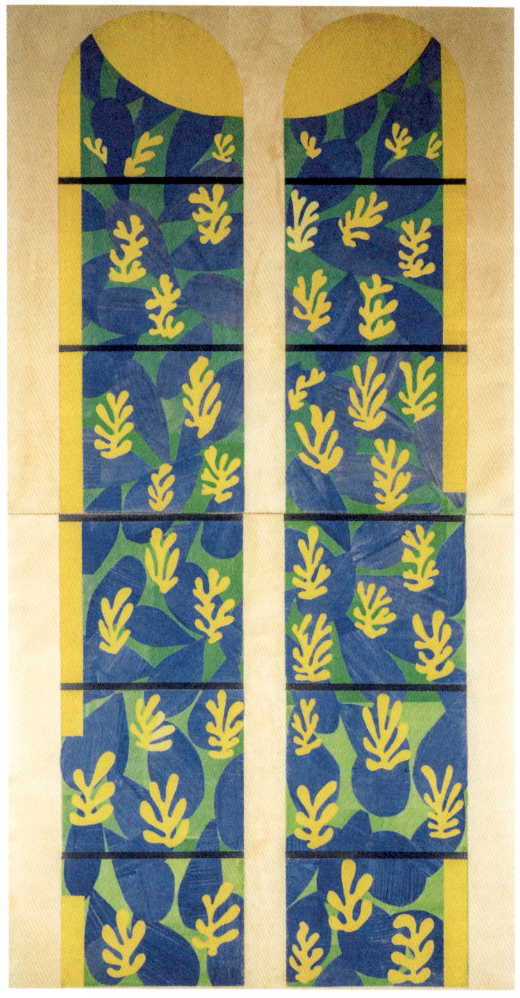

Tree of Life, 1949. Pasted papers enhanced with gouache and mounted on canvas, 509.8 × 252.3 cm (200¾ × 99⅜ in.).

Do I believe in God? Yes, when I am working. When I am receptive and humble.

I come from the North. You cannot imagine how I detested those dark churches.

The Chapel of the Rosary ... is the product of my entire working life. I consider it my masterpiece ... the result of a life dedicated to the pursuit of truth.

When I enter the chapel, I feel as if my whole self is here – or the best of me, the qualities I had as a child, and which I've tried to hold on to all my life.

Inside Notre-Dame-de-Paris ... a sea of heads, the architecture, the stained glass, waves of music from the organ.... What is my chapel, compared with that?... A flower. Just a flower, but a flower all the same.

The thing is to lose yourself and fly.

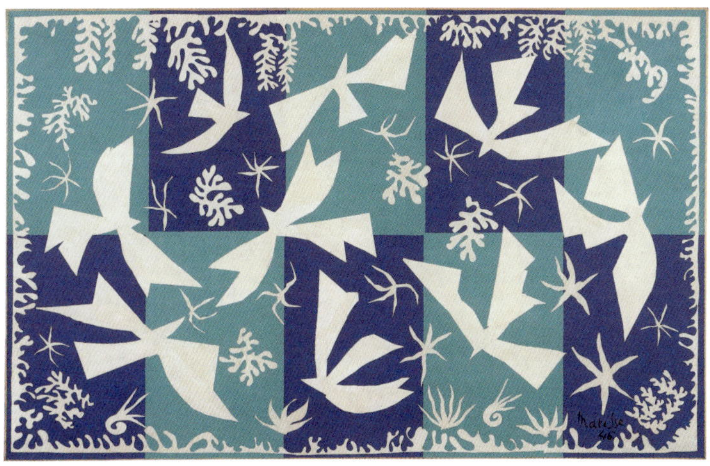

Polynesia, The Sky, 1946. Pasted papers enhanced with gouache and mounted on canvas, 200 × 314 cm (78¾ × 123⅝ in.).

How comforting ... if, after their death, those who gave their lives to developing their natural gifts for the good of all attained perfect satisfaction.

Work, be at peace. Beware of strong feelings.

Do not get set in your ways, stuck in a rut. It is important to get out and retemper your energies.

Leave the past behind.

An artist cannot go backwards without walking into Death. He must keep moving forwards.

Death is not the end of everything. It's a door that opens.

What an artist says matters so little, compared with what an artist does.

BIOGRAPHY

1869
Birth of Henri-Émile Benoît Matisse on 31 December, in the northern French town of Le Cateau-Cambrésis.

1888
Studies law and passes his first professional exams.

1890
Receives a box of paints during a bout of appendicitis, and begins copying colour prints.

1894
Moves to Paris to study art. Takes rooms with his lover Camille Joblaud at 19 quai Saint-Michel. Birth of their daughter Marguerite, 31 August.

1895
Admitted to the École des Beaux-Arts, in the studio of painter Gustave Moreau (1826–1898). Fellow pupils include lifelong friends André Rouveyre, Georges Rouault, and Albert Marquet. Makes his first visit to Belle-Île, off the coast of southern Brittany.

1897–8
Separates from Camille Joblaud. Meets and marries Amélie Parayre, who agrees to raise Marguerite. Honeymoon in London and Corsica.

1899–1900
Births of sons Jean Gérard (10 January 1899) and Pierre (13 June 1900).

1903–4
Two paintings accepted for the Salon d'Automne in Paris. Has his first one-man exhibition at the Galerie Vollard, Paris. Spends the summer of 1904 in Saint-Tropez, with the neo-Impressionist/Divisionist painters Paul Signac and Henri Cross.

1905
Summer in Collioure (south west France) with André Derain. Birth of the 'Fauve' style ('wild beasts' – so named as a critical slur of their work). Sarah and Michael Stein become his first American collectors. *Luxe, Calme et Volupté* (p. 161) is shown at the Salon des Indépendants, Paris.

1906–7
Travels to Algeria, Italy, and Collioure.

1908
Accepts students at his workshop in Paris. Publishes 'Notes of a Painter' in *La Grande Revue*.

1909
Moves with his family to a house in Issy-les-Moulineaux, south-west of Paris, and builds a studio in the grounds.

1910
Retrospective at Galerie Bernheim-Jeune, Paris. Winter in Spain (Granada, Madrid).

1911–12
Travels to Moscow to visit patrons Sergei Shchukin and Ivan Morosov. Extended stay in Morocco.

1914
Moves to a bigger apartment at 19 quai Saint-Michel. Refused for military service, at the age of forty-four.

1917–19
Takes rooms and a studio in Nice, eventually settling at 1 place Charles-Félix, near the seafront. Produces stage designs and costumes for Sergei Diaghilev's Ballets Russes.

1921
Exhibits in the United States, at the Carnegie International Exhibition in Pittsburgh.

1923–9
Major exhibitions in Moscow, New York City, and Copenhagen.

1924
Pierre Matisse moves to New York, where he becomes an influential art dealer.

1925
Matisse is made a chevalier of the Légion d'honneur.

1929–30
Turns sixty and travels to Tahiti via New York, Chicago, Los Angeles, and San Francisco. American collector Albert C. Barnes commissions a mural on the theme of dance, for his foundation in Pennsylvania.

1931–2
His first one-man show at the Museum of Modern Art, New York, opens. His first *livre d'artiste*, the *Poésies de Stéphane Mallarmé*, is published by Albert Skira.

1933
Installation of Matisse's mural *The Dance* at the Barnes Foundation, after reworking due to incorrect measurements. His former studio assistant Lydia Omeltchenko is hired as a companion nurse to Amélie. Lydia divorces and takes her maiden name, Delectorskaya, in 1936.

1935
Illustrates James Joyce's *Ulysses* for the Limited Editions Club of New York.

1937
Works by Matisse feature in the *Degenerate Art* exhibition staged by the Nazi Party in Munich and across Germany and Austria. Uses paper cut-out technique to create sets and costumes for Léonide Massine's ballet *Rouge et Noir*, with music by Dmitri Shostakovitch.

1938
Moves to a studio apartment in the former Hôtel Régina in Cimiez, overlooking Nice and the Mediterranean.

1939
Lydia Delectorskaya is dismissed by Amélie, attempts suicide but recovers, and escapes Paris with Matisse ahead of the Nazi invasion. The pair travel together to Nice via St-Jean-de-Luz in France's Basque country.

1940
Matisse and Amélie separate. Matisse refuses a number of opportunities to escape the war in France and leave for Brazil or New York.

1941
Intestinal surgery in a Lyon clinic severely impacts Matisse's health and mobility.

1941–4
Works in Nice, on paintings, drawings, and *livres d'artiste*, with art-school friend André Rouveyre as editorial adviser. Publishes *Dessins: Thèmes et Variations* in 1943 with a text by the banned Communist poet Louis Aragon. Creates paper cut-out collages for his book *Jazz*.

1943
Moves inland to the villa Le Rêve, Vence.

1944
Arrests of Marguerite and Amélie as agents in the French Resistance. Marguerite is tortured but escapes deportation at the German border and returns to Paris.

1945
Major retrospective of thirty-seven paintings at the Salon d'Automne, Paris. Exhibition of works by Matisse and Picasso at London's Victoria and Albert Museum.

1947
Promoted to commander of the Légion d'honneur. Begins designs for the architecture, interior, stained glass, and vestments of the Chapel of the Rosary in Vence, thanks to a former night nurse, Monique Bourgeois, ordained as Sister Jacques-Marie in the town's Dominican convent. Publication of *Jazz* with Matisse's own, handwritten text.

1949
Returns to the Hôtel Régina in Cimiez.

1950
First prize for painting at the Venice Biennale.

1951
Consecration of the Chapel of the Rosary. Alfred Barr's seminal study *Matisse: His Art and His Public* published by the Museum of Modern Art, New York.

1952
Opening of the Musée Henri Matisse in Le Cateau-Cambrésis.

1953
Major exhibition of paper cut-outs at Galerie Berggruen, Paris.

1954
Death of Henri Matisse on 3 November. Burial in Cimiez's hilltop cemetery, in a plot donated by the City of Nice.

SOURCES

Apollinaire, Guillaume, *Henri Matisse 1907–1918* (Paris: L'Echoppe, 1993)

Aragon, Louis, *Henri Matisse, roman, volumes I and II* (Paris: Gallimard, 1971)

Clair, Jean and Antoine Terrasse, *Bonnard, Matisse: Correspondance, 1925–1946* (Paris: Gallimard, 1991)

Billot, Marcel (ed.), *Henri Matisse, M.-A. Couturier, L.-B. Rayssiguier: La Chapelle de Vence, Journal d'une création* (Paris: Les Editions du Cerf, 1993)

Delectorskaya, Lydia, *Contre Vents et Marées* (Paris: Éditions Irus et Vincent Hansma, 1996)

Finsen, Hanne (ed.), *Matisse, Rouveyre, Correspondance* (Paris: Flammarion, 2001)

Fourcade, Dominique (ed.), *Henri Matisse: Écrits et propos sur l'Art* (Paris: Hermann, 1972)

Grammont, Claudine (ed.), *Correspondance entre Charles Camoin et Henri Matisse* (Lausanne: La Bibliothèque des Arts, 1997)

Grammont, Claudine (ed.), *Matisse-Marquet: Correspondance 1898–1947* (Lausanne: La Bibliothèque des Arts, 2008)

Grammont, Claudine (ed.), *Tout Matisse* (Paris: Éditions Robert Laffont, 2018)

Guilbaut, Serge, (ed.), *Henri Matisse, Bavardages: Les entretiens égarés, propos recueillis par Pierre Courthion* (Paris: Skira, 2017)

Lemny, Doïna, (ed.), *Matisse – Pallady et la Blouse Romaine: Deux artistes sous la censure. Correspondance* (Lyon: Fage Éditions, 2019)

Matisse, Henri, *Jazz* (Paris: Tériade, 1947)

Correspondence between Henri Matisse and Pierre Matisse, 1919–1954, Pierre Matisse Gallery Archives, The Morgan Library and Museum, New York

Correspondence between Henri Matisse and Marguerite Matisse, Archives Marguerite Matisse. Quoted in *Matisse et Marguerite, Le Regard d'un Père*, exhibition catalogue (Paris: Musée d'Art Moderne de Paris, 2025)

Munck, Jacqueline (ed.), *Matisse-Rouault, Correspondance 1906–1953* (Lausanne: La Bibliothèque des Arts, 2013)

Schneider, Pierre, *Matisse*, new edition (Paris: Flammarion, 2002)

Spurling, Hilary, *The Unknown Matisse* (London: Hamish Hamilton, 1998) and *Matisse: The Master* (London: Hamish Hamilton, 2005)

All translations by Louise Rogers Lalaurie

CAPTIONS AND CREDITS

Matisse quotation on cover: Finsen, Hanne (ed.), *Matisse, Rouveyre, Correspondance* (Paris: Flammarion, 2001), p. 650
Cover, page 156: *Icarus*, plate VIII from the illustrated book *Jazz*, 1947. Pochoir print on paper, 41.9 × 64 cm (16½ × 25¼ in.).
Endpapers: *Landscape at Collioure*, 1905 (detail, page 27).
Page 2: *Masque (self-portrait)*, 1945. Lithograph on Arches wove paper, 38.3 × 28.5 cm (15⅛ × 11¼ in.).
Page 12: *Young Sailor II*, 1906. Oil on canvas, 101.3 × 83 cm (39⅞ × 32¾ in.).
Page 24: *Self-Portrait in Shirtsleeves*, 1900. Oil on canvas, 64 × 45 cm (25¼ × 17¾in.).
Page 54: *The Painter and His Model*, 1916–17. Oil on canvas, 146.5 × 97 cm (57⅝ × 38¼ in.).
Page 88: *Marguerite with a Black Cat*, 1910. Oil on canvas, 94 × 64 cm (37 × 25¼ in.).
Page 106: *Large Red Interior*, 1948. Oil on canvas, 146 × 97 cm (57½ × 38¼ in.).
Page 120: *Entrance to the Kasbah*, 1912. Oil on canvas, 116 × 80 cm (45⅝ × 31½ in.).
Page 138: *Femme au chapeau (Woman with a Hat)*, 1905. Oil on canvas, 80.8 × 59.7 cm (31¾ × 23½ in.).
Page 146: *Self-Portrait*, 1941. Sanguine chalk on paper, 48 × 37.5 cm (19 × 14⅞ in.).

Images are listed by page number.

2, 19, 44, 45, 57, 58, 61, 71, 83, 122, 146: Private Collection; **12**: The Metropolitan Museum of Art, New York; **5**: Photo Art Resource/Scala, Florence. The Metropolitan Museum of Art, New York; **15, 32, 52, 54, 66, 87, 88, 106, 156, 161, 169**: Centre Pompidou, MNAM-CCI, Paris; **16, 20, 137**: Photo François Fernandez. Musée Matisse, Nice, Bequest of the Matisse heirs (inv. 63.2.74); **23**: Mildred Lane Kemper Art Museum, Washington University in St Louis; **endpapers, 27, 35, 27, 62,68, 72, 95, 126–7, 162**: Museum of Modern Art, New York; **28–9, 118**: The Barnes Foundation, Philadelphia; **38, 133**: Photo Philip Bernard/Musée départemental Matisse; **47**: Photo Nasjonalmuseet/Børre Høstland, Oslo; **48, 75, 154**: Musée des Beaux-Arts, Lyon; **65**: Ikeda Museum of 20th Century Art, Ito, Japan; **74**: Photo Bridgeman Images. Museum of Fine Arts Houston; **77**: Yale University Art Gallery; **78**: Museum of Fine Arts, Boston; **80–1, 143**: Baltimore Museum of Art; **84, 96, 99, 130**: The State Hermitage Museum, St Petersburg; **91**: Statens Museum for Kunst, SMK, Copenhagen; **92**: Musée Picasso, Paris; **100**: Photo Anne Hansteen. Nasjonalmuseet, Oslo; **105**: Photo Bridgeman Images. Baltimore Museum of Fine Arts; **109**: National Gallery of Art, Washington; **110**: Norton Simon Collection, Los Angeles; **113**: Pinacoteca Agnelli, Turin; **114, 120**: The Pushkin State Museum of Fine Arts, Moscow; **117**: Musée de Grenoble; **124**: Moderna Museet, Stockholm; **138**: Collection SFMOMA San Francisco Museum of Modern Art; **151**: Stedelijk Museum, Amsterdam; **166**: Photo Governorate of the Vatican City State-Directorate of the Vatican Museums

ABOUT THE AUTHOR
Louise Rogers Lalaurie is a writer and award-winning translator based between the Paris region and the UK. Her published translations include sixteen novels and more than thirty non-fiction titles covering the fine and decorative arts, design, and travel. She is the author of *Matisse: The Books* (Thames & Hudson).

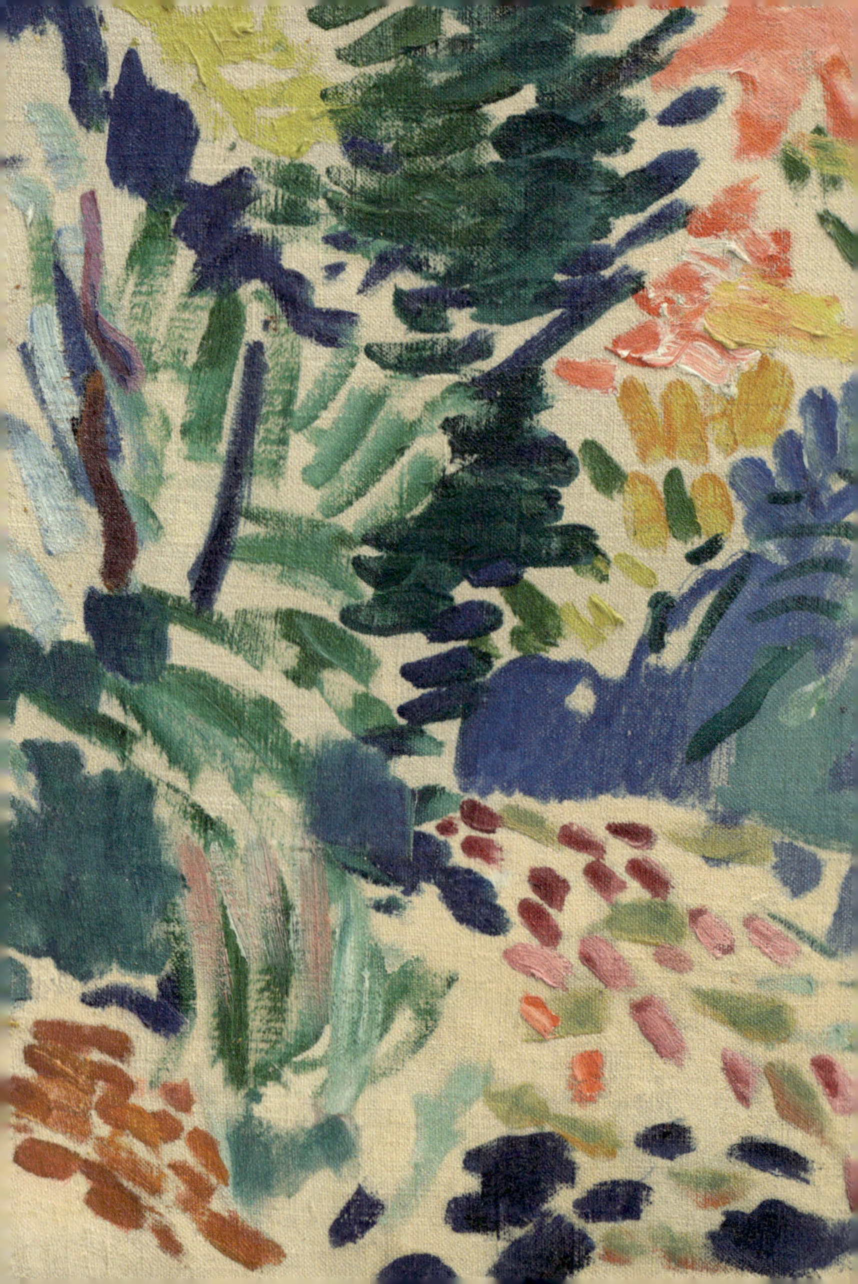